Children of The Second Birth

BEING A NARRATIVE OF SPIRITUAL
MIRACLES IN A CITY PARISH

By
S. M. SHOEMAKER, Jr.
Rector of Calvary Church in New York

". . . children of the second birth
Whom the world could not tame . . ."
—Matthew Arnold

New York   Chicago
Fleming H. Revell Company
London and Edinburgh

New York: 158 Fifth Avenue
Chicago: 851 Cass Street
London: 21 Paternoster Square
Edinburgh: 99 George Street

To the memory
of
THOMAS ALEXANDER LANGFORD
who gave his life
in the work at Calvary

"As for me, my bed is made. I am against bigness and greatness in all their forms, and with the invisible moral forces that work from individual to individual, stealing in through the crannies of the world like so many soft rootlets, or like the capillary oozing of water, and yet rending the hardest monuments of man's pride, if you give them time.

" The bigger the unit you deal with, the hollower, the more brutal, the more mendacious is the life displayed."

　　—WILLIAM JAMES, in a letter to Mrs. Henry Whitman.

" Nothing is more characteristic of Jesus' method than His indifference to the many—His devotion to the single soul. His attitude to the public, and His attitude to a private person were a contrast and a contradiction. If His work was likely to cause a sensation, Jesus charged His disciples to let no man know it: if the people got wind of Him, He fled to solitary places: if they found Him, as soon as might be He escaped. But He used to take young men home with Him, who wished to ask questions: He would spend all night with a perplexed scholar: He gave an afternoon to a Samaritan woman. He denied Himself to the multitude: He lay in wait for the individual. This was not because He under-valued a thousand, it was because He could not work on the thousand scale; it was not because He over-valued the individual, it was because His method was arranged for the scale of one."

　　—JOHN WATSON, *The Mind of the Master*.

"Again and again, before our time, men have grown content with a diluted doctrine. And again and again there has followed on that dilution, coming as out of the darkness in a crimson cataract, the strength of the red original wine."

　　—G. K. CHESTERTON, *The Everlasting Man*.

CONTENTS

I

AN ADVENTURE IN APOSTOLIC CHRISTIANITY

IN a moment of enthusiasm one day, during a conversation on the telephone, I told a fragment of one of the stories which follows; and the friend at the other end said, " Why don't you print that story in full? I am sure that things like that don't happen in our church."

For better or for worse I have taken the suggestion and committed that story, and some others like it, to " the dreadful perpetuity of print." For better, if some persons can be led by these stories into a vision of dry bones (personal or ecclesiastical) turning into life; for worse, if any one can read through these stories of human deliverance, yet miss the throbbing meaning of it all, and feel that it is nothing to them.

Some will probably say that these stories are too intimate to publish. I have my moods like that, too. If any one has the right to feel that the things here set down are too revealing for paper and printer's ink, it is I myself; for from the beginnings, through high and low points in the pilgrimage, I have shared with these friends the experiences of the spiritual journey thus far. I respect

9

them as perhaps one only can who is permitted the privilege of spiritual intimacy. I least of all would wish to have publicity brush a touch of the bloom from the naturalness and radiant spiritual joy and simplicity of them.

But they and I belong to a new generation, which is feverishly trying to find its way to fullness of life. The human mind has been turned upside down these last few years; and in the cellars of it we have been finding some things of which we cannot afford to be very proud. We have found ourselves pretty dishonest, pretty raw, pretty animal about a good many things. And some people are therefore trying to be honest, and reasonable about the human equipment, trying to face life as it is, and see what we can do with it.

We who stand behind these stories, and vouch for the experiences which are here recorded, believe that the deep hungers of the spirit for traffic with the Unseen, the longing for spiritual wholeness and unity and satisfaction, are also part and parcel of human nature, demanding to be heard from and reckoned with as much as any physical instinct. Some of us wandered long before we fully admitted that. But, like honest Tolstoi, we died when we denied it, and we lived when we recognized it. We tell these stories for what they are worth. They ought to have upon them the brand of actual, first-hand experience. We offer them to those who will read them for the simple reason that we have found a way of life which fully and entirely satisfies, and we do not care to keep it to ourselves. We believe that whatever has the possibility of helping somebody, has the warrant to be made public.

These spiritual adventures took place in connection with the work of an old, downtown church in the middle of New York City. Business roars around us; Gramercy Park is a little residential oasis to the east of us. I mention our locality, not because geography much affects grace—these stories might just as well have taken place on great uptown avenues if some who are too much at ease in Zion should grow warm with concern about themselves, and demand a more challenging and vital spiritual experience; but I have hopes this book may carry a new vision to some who work under the circumstances of a somewhat faded neighbourhood, and help them to see that their limitations may be blessings in disguise.

By their limitations, they may be forced to forego the worship of the god of numbers, and turn to doing spiritual work with individuals. Jesus seems to me to have chosen between touching slightly a whole countryside, and influencing deeply a handful. He took the handful. And I believe enough in the moral character of God, in His faith in quality against quantity, to think that some day He may cause our reports and our categories of magnitude to look very ridiculous indeed:

and gravely embarrass us by asking us why we mourned the smallness of our numbers, instead of vitalizing the spiritually mediocre who may have sat beneath our preaching for years.

I hope through the pages of this book to say something to some of my brothers in the ministry and in other full-time religious work. A good many of them tell me, in the honesty of intimacy, that they feel they have slipped from the high vision they had of the work when they went into it. I would like to remind such preachers as say they do not find time for personal work, that the Saviour of the world found time for it, and thought that it would help to win the world if He sat on the coping of a well and talked to a town-woman until she was changed and became a bearer of good tidings to a city.

Some men in the ministry, to-day, are parched and living at second-hand, prisoned with books in their studies till they have no time to read men, slaving over great organizations and missing the needs of the elevator-boy who takes them to the office, touching thousands at arm's length from a pulpit, but coming to close grips with almost none. I know that such men are not satisfied. They must know that their public work would be better for a testing of their message in private, clinically.

And every time I see the burden put upon them by administration and money-raising and executive detail, I ask myself whether *all* this is really necessary, whether some of it may not be just an attempt to seem busy, something to make them feel the motions of a success which in their hearts they fear they are not really having. These may sound like hard words; but I sometimes come behind the scenes in such lives, and for sheer, blank tragedy I know nothing like a man for whom the Gospel has gotten cold, and who has taken refuge in activity round the fringes of it.

But perhaps most of all, I am after the outsider. I talk with him every day of my life. I know his prejudices and his power to see our weaknesses; and I know also that inner love for Christ which is his, and his admiration of those who really live Christ's kind of life. He is not able to understand much of our theology, he is fuddled by our ritual and funny little tame church-ways, he is aghast at what he considers our pretense and humbug and the quarrelsomeness amongst ourselves. But he understands it when a bad man turns good, or when a good man shakes off his self-satisfaction and becomes Christian. He understands it when a man on the road to nowhere finds a direction towards a destiny, or when a life adrift comes into harbour—he understands and he likes it, and he says in the soul of him: " Now, that's what I call Christianity."

There is no more scathing proof that most of us Christians are off the track than the judgment of the outsider who secretly loves the Lord Jesus, as all normal men do, but feels us so faithless in our following, so impotent and unenthusiastic in our witness, that he does not care to fall into step with us. Jesus was always conscious of the outsiders. They liked Him, felt at home with Him. Out of them He made His great forces, turning the energy of their opposition and sin into the energy of loyalty and support.

Through the streets of the city are thousands who I wish might know of these changed and transformed lives—thousands who are heart-hungry and lonely and tired of sin and at war with themselves and making a failure of life. One of them often tells me of the hunger of the rest. And I have noticed that really vital religion sometimes goes straight over the heads of merely nominal Christians—the present-day Pharisees— and hits these dear old publicans and sinners in the solar plexus, just as it did of old. I'd give anything to fetch more of them in, and get them to see that they also can become finders of life.

I hope the book will not sound presumptuous. The thing is a witness, and I have not spared personal pronouns when they add emphasis. There is something perhaps which is finally and innately dogmatic about all actual experience; it happens, and what happens is a fact, and you can't budge facts. When a man says, " Whereas I was blind, now I see," there is an end of argument. When the whole life testifies to the change, there is no appeal from that. It is as immovable as a mountain, as fixed as the stars.

I am aware that there is nothing new in any story I shall tell. Things like these have happened ever since Christ came. Across the world there are individuals and little groups that are doing the same kind of thing—though there are not so very many of them. Experiences like this take place wherever men go back to the New Testament and try to make its principles a working force in their world. But you must not be surprised if men and women who have had the experience tell of it with something of a startled and delighted surprise. The type of event may be old; but the event itself is new, and comes into their lives trailing such clouds of joy that they tell of it as if no man had ever found God before.

Of course these stories are not ended, because the people are still alive. Therefore they will change. Some of them will go forward, some may even go backward. The only people I know who will not change are dead people. Plenty of men and women have " stuck " for years. Some have slipped back, and are now miserable because of what they once saw. If they get miserable enough, they will come back. None of us arrives in this world; we are travelling. But the people in these stories seem to me to be travelling in a fruitful direction and to know where they are going. If they are like the rest of us, there await them battles and persecutions and misunderstandings and some ups and downs; but so also do greater discoveries and growing assurance and the perpetual and undiminishing joy of seeing others grow as a result of their witness.

The narratives in this book prove the statement of William James, that " Self-surrender . . . always must be regarded as the vital turning-point of the religious life." We believe entirely that conversion is the experience which initiates the new life. But we are not fools enough to think that the beginning is the end! All subsequent life is a development of the relationship with God which conversion opened. For us its daily focal-point is in what we call the " Quiet Time." As in all other private devotions, we pray and read the Bible. But the distinguishing element of a Quiet Time is listening for the guidance of God. " Speak, Lord, for Thy servant heareth," is the expectant mood of a Quiet Time. The validity of what we believe to be God's guidance must show itself, in the long run, by more acute moral perception, more genuine human relationships, and increasing assurance of what one ought to do with every hour of the day.

I only hope that these stories breathe life, and make religion seem alive and attractive and workable. All of us who have had part in writing them will be well enough rewarded if only a few are helped towards Christ by what we have written.

II

WHAT THE LAW COULD NOT DO

THIS story is of a college graduate, a son of privilege, who was born into a family of cultivated and well-to-do Jewish parents. If you could see the gay and irrepressible spirits of this man, and listen to his keen and ever-ready and kindly humour, and watch him take life in long, easy strides, you would not believe that for years he was devilled with such a sense of inferiority as made him almost despair of himself, or with a still worse demon of lust which carried him on till he had gone the pace with the worst. No man was ever born with a greater inner necessity for fine living than he. And few have tried more assiduously to drown out such inward need by ridicule, by bad company, and by sin. I think that he could say with all the truth in the world what that unfortunate and hapless parson, William Dodd, said just before he came to his untimely end for his wrongdoing: "I have always sinned against conviction."

Less than two years ago this figure presented himself at my door. He carried an introduction from a friend of mine, which said that he was "having a hard time with himself." The lines in his face told of inner worry. A furtive glance, something shy and fearful and uneasy, impressed me at once. So did intelligence, a ready mind, and a kind heart. During a talk of five hours his story came out. And it is this:

His earliest recollection of happiness is the remembrance of following his mother about, and having her call him her shadow, or " Stick-in-the-Mud." He clung to her desperately.

By seven or eight he was conscious of not being a well-rounded average American boy. He greatly disliked all competition in athletic games. He was afraid of them, and of boys who played them well.

At the age of about fourteen began the terrible struggles of adolescence, aggravated for him because he knew nothing of the power of religion. " The depth of evil in my desires," he says, " no one would have suspected then, few would believe now."

At sixteen he was sent off to a great preparatory school. During the first few days he heard himself being talked over, in that casual, cruel manner of schoolboys; they agreed that this new boy was " not the sort of fellow that's easy to talk to." " Here began my conscious inferiority," he relates. " Those words rung and resounded in my ears all through school and college, made me embarrassed every time I met people, and had their part, I believe, in keeping me out of a fraternity at college. There were so few places where I felt at home that I cannot even remember where they were. I didn't for years find my element. I stayed by myself, leaned against the fireplace in the common-room, watched the school go on round me, and felt sorry for myself."

If anyone has the imagination to know the anguish that lies behind those words, they will realize that for a sensitive child it is an extremely difficult thing to get from twelve to twenty.

"In school I got my first 'spurt' of religion. There were beautiful services which æsthetically I loved. I liked the hymns, and one especially touched me very deeply, which ran:

> ' As of old St. Andrew heard it,
>   By the Galilean lake,
>   Turned from home and toil and kindred,
>   Leaving all for His dear sake.'

I used to wonder if I could ever hear that call.

"In this school I met a man whom I set high on a pedestal. He was one of the masters. He has been a friend through thick and thin, taking me into his family and giving me of himself, until he was for eight years the greatest influence in my life. It is strange that such a good friend, being such an ideal example, did so little to make me better. His example was not enough.

"Then came college. I made a name for myself in dramatics, and began parties and drinking—and the things that go with them. But in

my heart were the unsteady ups-and-downs of an
uncentered life. I was a slave to changing moods.
Later on, I met the rector of the Episcopal church,
who was agreeable and sympathetic, and I have
continued to count on his friendship. We had
long talks together.

" But my religion amounted to this—that heaven
and hell are on earth, and that God is the wee
small voice within.

" They had instituted a system of 'personal
ratings' in the college, and I ranked very low in
' reliability.' All this time the vilest of imaginings were filling my mind. And in the spring of
junior year the crash came; I had been caught
in the act, and I was called to the dean's office. In
a curious way, I was rather thankful that I had
been caught. These terrible sins had been shut
within my own soul, and I was not sorry to have a
chance to make a clean breast of it with a man I
could trust. I was anything but defiant, and told
him everything."

Then followed an interview with the president,
who said the college wanted to help him if he
wanted to be helped, and he was sent to a famous
psychiatrist during Easter vacation. He went with
full confidence that he could be helped.

The psychiatrist told him that if he did come
out in the end, he would have developed a wonderful will! " If "—where it was his business to turn
that " if " into " when "! Imagine a man telling

a boy to develop his will, when for years he had been trying to ward off failure, defeat, setbacks! He was told to try to be less self-conscious, and more sociable—as if he had not been " trying " till it hurt. He was to acquire a hobby. And science, *per se*, knew nothing of what to do with a powerful physical urge, save to give in to it.

He writes: " Then the little religion I seemed to have had apparently passed out of my life altogether. I regretted its passing; I still had some sort of a faith, but it was very vague and uncertain."

At this time there occurred two experiences which destroyed the idealism which he had always felt about women. With something instinctive he continued, indeed, to cling to his mother—but his faith in women in general, and in the ideal of marriage, was shattered.

He had lost moral grip. He lost grip on his studies, too.

It would be well sometimes if professors and ministers realized more fully how the evil in a man's life helps to create the doubt in his mind. The kind of life this man was living was a very natural matrix for his kind of thinking. I do not say that all doubt is caused by sin alone; I say that much of it is. And I believe that, by as much as none of us is free from sin, and sin is always calling to doubt, " Come over and help us," by so much is the doubt of every unbeliever affected, consciously or unconsciously, by those things in his life of which God cannot possibly approve. I have never found doubt unalloyed by sin, because I have never found a human being who was not a sinner.

To resume the story: There followed two and a half years of unsuccessful attempts to stick at a variety of jobs. Then something happened which caused a significant turn in his affairs. The Episcopal rector, who had kept steadily in touch with him, wrote him to get hold of Harold Begbie's *More Twice-Born Men*. He got it, and read it. It was entirely new to him. What helped him most were certain passages which made him realize that to get in step with the evolution of the universe he had to get in step with God; and that sin was anything, and the only thing, that walled men away from God. This was his first concrete idea of what constitutes sin.

Nevertheless, he drifted back to the city, to a life more evil and unhappy than ever, to a job dull and uninspiring. He thought nothing of the book or of Christ for a year. He tried to kill his conscience. He saw other men living rotten lives and seemingly suffering no remorse. One night he fetched up in a negro dance-hall in Harlem, drunk as a loon, entertaining the spectators by making an exhibition of himself as a solo-dancer.

But he found it difficult to be a successful gentleman-bum; that is, a happy one. Conscience persisted, no matter to what lengths he went nor for how long a time he tried to stifle it. It made him wonder again whether there was a God who wished him to become something better.

He was then twenty-four years old. The devotion of a mother, the opportunities which money affords, ideals held up in school, the system of education in a great university, the friendly admonitions of dean and president, skirting as they did the real root of the matter, the absurd and vicious guidance of a psychiatrist, and all the little unaccounted pressures of the life all about us—they had all brought him to this, having given the best they had. As Professor Hocking says,[1] "If I were to name the chief defect of contemporary education, it would not be that it turns out persons who believe and behave as their fathers did—it does not; but that it produces so many stunted wills, wills prematurely grey and incapable of greatness, not because of lack of endowment, but because they have never been searchingly exposed to what is noble, generous, and faith-provoking." Most of the products of our homes and schools and universities are too commonplace and contained, too material and inarticulate, to let us have a glimpse of these

" Desperate tides of the whole great world's anguish
    Forced through the channels of a single heart."

[1] *Human Nature and Its Remaking*, W. E. Hocking, p. 233.

It is only upon a soil as sensitive as the soul of this boy that we can get a fair register of the effect of such processes as surround our present-day youth, or understand the schemes and systems by which they are being ripened into manhood. That "something is lacking" is too tame a judgment. That these young men have been mildly but not "searchingly exposed" to religion with grip and grit in it, is the reason for their inner division, their want of purpose, their frequent moral deflection.

And now we come to the happier part of the story. When all this sad tale was gotten into the open, he asked me what was the way out for him. I said that I could tell him of a Christ who could actually save men from their sins, put a new heart in them, and send them on their way rejoicing. He ⸱ dged for a moment on his own conception of Christ, saying that at present he could only feel Him the best Man that ever was. And I told him I thought that was a very good place to start; it was where the first apostles started when He called them away from the lakeside to become fishers of men. They knew nothing then of His divinity, all they knew was that they were irresistibly attracted by Him, felt He was unanswerably right about life, and were willing to drop everything to spread His way of life. As time wore on, their vision enlarged, their experience deepened, and they saw the whole Christ.

So he said that he would "surrender as much of himself as he could, to as much of Christ as he understood." It would be far better if we would let men begin their discipleship where they honestly can, letting their experiences develop until their theology comes straight, rather than cramming a creed down fellows' throats and thinking that it means anything to swallow it whole without digesting it.

I quote now from his diary: " Before I left, we got down on our knees in prayer together—a new and wonderful Christian experience for me—and I dedicated my life not only to belief in Jesus Christ, but to His life and work. The horrible and hated aspect of my past is falling away, as if belonging to another person. I do feel reborn, born of the Spirit."

We met and talked two or three times a week, and I could watch the lines grow fainter in his face, and a freedom and release he had never known before come to take their place. There had been something a little exhausting about him when he first came in; it wore me out to talk to him—I was tired when he went away. This steadily diminished, and I found him more companionable and interesting.

But about six weeks from the time of his conversion there began one of those slipping-times which none of us is stranger to. First the old imaginings returned, wretched pictures in his mind.

Then the slackening of prayer and of Quiet Time. Then the relaxing of the grip on the will and, finally, the fall. What you think of long enough, that you will almost inevitably do. In a conflict between will and imagination, imagination is likely to win in an unguarded moment. He slipped back with a terrible crash into the old ways.

Now, there will be some who will say that this is only what they expected—these sudden conversions never do last. But spiritual biography is full of men and women who have slipped, and slipped badly, soon after their conversion, and yet have turned again to God and made a winning fight. I introduce this incident because it may help some who have fallen since their conversion, and felt themselves hopeless. This was the *last failure* to avoid outbreaking sin in this man's life, and it happened nearly two years ago. The difference between the sin of a man before he is converted, and afterwards, has been most happily caught in a little dialect rhyme of the late Father Tabb, called " The Difference ":

> " Unc' Si, de Holy Bible say,
>   In speakin' of de jus',
>   Dat he do fall seb'n times a day:
>   Now, how's de sinner wuss?
>
> " ' Well, chile, de slip may come to all,
>   But den the diff'ence foller;
>   For ef you watch him when he fall,
>   De jus' man do not *waller.* ' "

That January we decided to have his baptism. It was a wonderful service. Throughout the autumn a little group of us had been gathering one evening a week to pray and think and talk together about winning men for Christ, and he was one of this group. It was an intimate fellowship, and he decided that he would like to receive baptism in the presence of that group. I shall never forget our having prayer together before the service; almost everyone prayed, and when it came the turn for our friend who was to be baptized, he broke out into a flood of praise to Christ, saying amongst other things, as if he had known the custom of the early Church: " I believe with all my heart that Jesus Christ is my Saviour."

In March he was confirmed, taking upon himself the final responsibilities of the Christian's life in the Church.

One sometimes feels, of a life like this, that God has long ago laid His hand upon it for a great end, and it is only a question of patience and obedience till His full plan for the mature labour of that life is made plain. This man hated to grub for money; he cared for people and ideas, not for things. All his interest centered in ideal things, not in material ones. Not that he despises material things; he enjoys all the normal pleasures of life, he is neat to the point of being almost a dandy at times. But the things that get hold of his heart are the things of the Spirit. It was therefore most natural that he should consider the possibility of his entering the ministry. And when I suggested to him that he become a member of our staff at the church for a time, and see how he got on with it, he jumped at it and was ready to come at any time.

One day, I had a call from some members of his family. They felt that his becoming a Christian might have been all right, the baptism explainable, the confirmation pardonable. But to burn all his bridges, to leave his place of business, to break with all his past life—this was too much; and I must realize what a shifty career he had had, always leaving this to take up that, and never staying by anything.

My reply took this form: He has stuck with us for eight months, he loves this work, his heart is in it. You say he has shifted about, and he has. But has any other interest he has met with done for him what this has done? Has anything else loosened his tensions, freed him of his complexes, released him from the terrific tug of the old life?

To this a brilliant sister replied: " I must admit, on simply psychological grounds, that you have freed him of all his old inhibitions." And I asked if they did not think it perfectly safe for him to invest his life in that which had saved his life.

Then with great honesty his mother said to her daughter: " N., this man is talking about something you and I know nothing about." There was a wistful appreciation in that remark; so wistful

and so appreciative that one hopes one day we
shall have her with us, and bring her into the
sealed fellowship with Christ at the same font
whither, with exquisitely loving thought, she followed her son on the day of his baptism.

And so, on April 1, he came to give his whole
life and work to Christ, and to working on our
staff.

Perhaps it is nowhere else so hard to share one's
inmost feelings and beliefs as with one's family;
and it is a great day when one has taken this decisive step. " Thank God for this day! " he writes.
" Coming home to-night, I felt the power of the
Spirit, and that it was a good time to tell the folks
about everything, all of them together. To-night
I cleared the air and burned all the bridges. I told
them just what had been happening these past two
days of working with people, and what my hopes
were for the future. I told them about having
had lunch downtown with J., who asked me why I
was looking so well and seemed such an amazingly
different person these last few months—which gave
me a wonderful opening. He saw that I had found
the real thing, and said so. Asked me how I kept
it, and was delighted to have me reply, ' By doing
just what I am doing now—talking to fellows like
you! ' He says he knows a fellow that needs it
more than he does, and wants to know if he could
convert somebody else without being converted
himself! "

Here are some of his convictions about those systematic times of waiting upon God which all Christian experience has found necessary, and also those inspirations which slip into our minds at all kinds of times through the day: " When one has been regular in morning Quiet Times, the days go off much better—which means everything in the day, work, enjoyment, health, spirit, less temptation—sleep better and stay awake better. I am all for concentrated and regular Quiet Times.

" One of the many things I have found to be true in my experience of this new life is the idea of ' driving stakes.' Every real talk with another person is a prop to hold me up straight. It is as if I were a tent-pole, and every talk with someone else were a stake round the outside. The more there are of them, the more likely is the pole to be held upright. I am not apt to slip, now when I can think of the many who are looking to me —some perhaps sceptically, to see if I shall fall, but others with faith, and relying on me for some strength."

I wish that there were space to record some of the conversations he has had with other individuals. I shall choose only three.

" There was M., who worked in the bank with me. One night, after an employes' dance, we rode in the park in an old hansom cab. Whether we should be tempted to go on a party, or whether we should meet on the best level, was soon determined, for he himself began to talk about religion. We shared our ideas of God and Christ, and I told of my change.

" And there was J., with whom I went on my last tear. It was hard to say anything after that. I wanted to undo the wrong. I prayed for the chance. For the first time I felt ready to face him, and as I was walking on downtown Broadway, he caught me by the arm. We talked a bit. He was anxious to see me after that, and hear more of the new life. I hope yet to win him finally.

" The most interesting piece of guidance of them all was what happened at the Three-Hours' Service on Good Friday. As I stood near the door, I noticed a tall, well-dressed fellow come in and sit in the rear of the church. Through the service I saw him at times moved to the point of suffering. Before the end, he got up to go out; and a strong urge told me to speak to him in the porch. For a moment I disobeyed, but then I followed him, saying simply: ' I don't think we have seen you here before, have we? ' He was touched that anyone spoke to him, aired his views of the stupid inhumanity of churches generally, and we talked about personal religion. He declares he does not want it. But he told another man in his office of this experience, and of what I had said to him. This second man came to one of our group meetings; he is an unordained Methodist preacher, and was soundly converted that day. He was tied in a hundred knots, worrying, anxious over his sermons, and defeated in his own life. We got it all out in the open, and he said he had never before preached as he did that next Sunday, and this freedom had not left him. The man who was in church that Good Friday tells me he is a ' barren field '; but to produce another man so early seems a fairly good first crop. And if he is so fruitless and unlikely a prospect, I wonder why he keeps coming around? "

When, on a certain Sunday in late June, a young man stood up in church to read the Scriptures, very few knew that this story of great spiritual deliverance lay behind him, and had brought him there. It was with no conventional monotony that he read those lessons, but his voice rang with personal conviction, personal desire to make every word " get over " to the very last pew in a large church. I think that teachers in elocution might spare themselves some pains, and our church people some misery, if they could only see to it that the readers were themselves converted in their inmost hearts, and read what they believed, " speaking that we do know," and were deeply concerned to impart to others. When this young lay-reader came that evening to the third chapter of St. John, I felt something almost electric in the air, as if Nicodemus had come to life in our midst, and stood there changed and transformed, testifying the great truth which he had heard from the Lord, " Ye *must* be born again."

On August 1 last, this man celebrated his first Christian anniversary by speaking at Calvary Mission. The words of one who was present and heard what he said tell very simply of this meeting: " A young Jew, the son of a successful banker, had known for a year what the new life is that Calvary demands of each one of us, and he celebrated with these men at the mission his anniversary of 365 days. He had been dissipated and bitterly unhappy. It may sound sensational, but it was the most simple, most honest and most moving occasion."

Sometimes, as I look at him, I seem to be unable to connect him with that old and beaten and badgered personality which used to inhabit his body. It is as though one person had moved out, and another one altogether had moved in—as though his body had had two separate tenants. I have never met a man more completely transformed. " The regret, the struggle, and the failing " seem to have belonged to someone else entirely—so free, so sane, so thoroughly sound and natural and happy and clean does he seem. And I apply to him the words of that other high-souled Jew who could find no peace in his own persuasion:

" For the law of the Spirit of life in Christ Jesus hath made me free from the law of sin and death.

" For what the law could not do, in that it was weak through the flesh, God sending his own Son

in the likeness of sinful flesh, and for sin, con-
demned sin in the flesh: that the righteousness of
the law might be fulfilled in us, who walk not after
the flesh, but after the Spirit." [1]

[1] St. Paul's Epistle to the Romans, Chapter 8, verses 2–4.

III

" I DID—AND IT DOES! "

THIS is the story of a man in whom in-feriority had become so ingrained that it very nearly destroyed all happiness and meaning in living—and who has found the Way Out.

He is a most winsome personality, a good athlete, with a smile that can take the chill off a winter's day. Nobody would ever suspect the suffering and self-distrust which has lain behind the happy exterior of this man.

Some months before, he had heard an address at Princeton, and he came to the city thinking I might give him some help. In talking with him, I soon found that the problem was one of basic adjustment to life. He showed a deep discontent with himself and his family and his achievements. His talk rang with the harshest of self-judgment. But one found also the ever-present " compensation "—the feeling of " superiority " over other people in certain respects, upon which he could dwell with temporary satisfaction.

It seemed wise to have the help of science in attempting to eradicate his trouble, and so we sought out a good psychiatrist, a man very different from the doctor mentioned in "What the Law Could Not Do." He is a man of the highest character himself, and one who believes in the workability of the finest of ideals. Together he and I have discussed this man's problems with him—a triangular relationship of genuine friendship and understanding. Science has dealt with the mental and physical facts; religion has supplied the new motive, and surrounded him with the atmosphere of faith. I doubt if either science or religion, single-handed, could have won the day; but together they have done it. And here is a parable for all scientists who fear religion, and all religionists who fear science.

He needed constant companionship, and so he came to stay with me for several weeks. I doubt if he had two whole hours of real happiness during the entire time. He did not like to go out, for he might meet his friends, and they would not understand why he was not at work. A movie might divert him for a few hours—or perhaps a walk, or a game of golf. But it was necessary very often to drop everything, to be ready to talk with him. That alone seemed to give relief—to let him talk it out, and go into all the little repetitious details as often as he cared to, saying to him encouraging things about himself which he could not really take in. He often made the distinction between the things he "knew" and the things he "felt"; there were plenty of the first class, few of the

second—and it was the second which alone put
power and meaning into life. These were weeks
of intense difficulty for him. But he had found two
people to whom he could talk without reserve, and
whom he knew to be interested in him for his own
sake; he " knew " it, and occasionally he " felt " it.

Then followed two years at home. Part of the
tragedy of a situation like this is that those nearest to us are the first to be estranged from us.
Adjustment with the family was almost impossible
for him. He worked in his father's business, and
did extremely well. But still there was not much
meaning to his work, no inner sense of significance or joy.

There was not one particle of objective reality
in his strictures against his own flesh and blood.
His parents were not critical of him, nor expecting
too much, nor unreasonable. On the contrary, they
have throughout been most generous and understanding of him, ready to make any sacrifices for
him, coöperative to the last degree with us who
were helping their son. No boy ever had better
parents—all the trouble came from his own attitude, but over that attitude he had not yet found
control.

He made two long trips, seeking satisfaction in
new sights and new occupations, and finding some.
But still there was home to be faced again, and
the family, and what to do, and all the dragging
hours of days empty of real meaning.

Last summer he turned up again in the city. He was staying in a hotel, spending hours reading the newspapers, keeping to himself, seeking solitary occupations, finding scant and temporary pleasure in a few friends. He wanted to support himself; he wanted to make good. But resolution was balked and thwarted by insufficient energy and inadequate motive. Everything ended in boredom. Nothing mattered.

I suggested that he come down with us, for there were certain kinds of work for which he had the strength and the capacity. He came. He did as much as he could, and the amount increased as the interest increased.

At first religion was just a " value " to him. It had not objective substantial existence, it only became alive to people because they " believed " in it. But he stayed about. He met a great many kinds of people, all undergoing the transforming experience of religion. Some did not interest him at all, others were of his own intellectual calibre and drew him to them. Living in the staff-house, he found for the first time a perfectly sympathetic milieu—everyone wanted to help him, and he could see that undoubtedly things were happening in other peoples' lives.

One day he began getting " guidance." It came in such simple, elemental flashes to him that its crystal-clearness struck us all. His spoken prayers in the group had in them a childlike quality that was profoundly beautiful and comprehensive.

He has taught us all much about guidance in the details of life. During the winter, he got overtired and had to take a rest; it came from overconscientiousness in his work, which caused him to do much more than he should have done. "It was all against my guidance," he said later. "It was clear to me often that I should stop work, and rest; but everybody else was going on, and I thought I could, too. But it doesn't work to disobey guidance."

Many people, on *a priori* and ill-considered grounds, think that divine guidance will drive them to constant exertion, lash them into nervous activity, keep their nose ever to the grindstone; that it means only submission to the sharpest demands of over-developed consciences. But far otherwise is the case. Many are the times when God commands rest, relaxation, or pleasure. There are few lives in our generation over-driven by conscience; but for them there is written a very wonderful verse in the Scripture: ". . . If our heart condemn us, God is greater than our heart, and knoweth all things." This man has taught us that God lays upon men no burdens greater than they can carry—and that He warns, when the strain is growing too heavy. It takes many lives to round out the whole experience of guided living, to show the divine normality of the God-led life.   Some lives God rouses and shakes, and some lives God quiets and comforts.   He gives what we need.

When he went home for vacation, things were different.   The old surroundings were there.   Anyone who knows the human mind knows that the scenes of struggle always bring back the memory of it.   It would have been easy to have a time of depression and slump—but it did not come.   One day he spoke in the church at home—and enjoyed the ordeal!   The family took a personal interest in the kind of religion he was finding.   So did his friends.   The visit at home was a victory; he came back with a different feeling about the family and all that they stood for.

Steadily his inner life has been developing.   He is finding pleasure where before any occupation was as dry as straw.   He is discovering value where emptiness had seemed unendurable.   " I have found two things," he says.   " God exists, and He can really help me."   He has found those realities through the friendship of believing people, through an atmosphere charged with positive faith about life, and definite and specific hope, about him, and through love which understands and has plenty of time and is patient and expectant.   To the group he contributes something which no one else contributes.   His work is effective.   It is a pleasure to have him about the house.   And it is a joy to see a life shake off the shackles of the past, and find its way into the future with confidence and peace.

At a Mission of Personal Witness for Christ, he gave his testimony, with some twenty others. His notes for that talk are so revealing that I give them just as he wrote them down:

" Brought up in Christian home. Outwardly acquiescent. Attended Sunday School and Church, excelled in lessons, deportment, attitude towards teachers, etc.

" As soon as able to do so, stopped flat in attending Sunday School, and later Church. Services at ——————— School and Princeton meant nothing to me, as a help; when interesting, they served same purpose for me as a lecture—informative.

" Stoical. Alone. Hated more and more any semblance of worship. Devoured all material opposing Christianity, or any religion, as hypocritical superstition. Tried to fight alone—a failure.

" A terrible pang there. Hate of the mention or sight of worship spread as an infection to all things, to people, to friends. Against my will and my strongest efforts were engendered suspicions, envy, hate and irritability, despondency and loss of hope. Outwardly calm, inwardly stricken.

" Opportunities rejected secular and spiritual. Finally, this summer still distraught in mind, decided to try Christianity—*real* Christianity, experimentally.

" One thing after another has bloomed. A great yawning void that hurt like a sore tooth, has been filled and is filling daily. First, guidance—then a new real happiness, the only one. New meaning to meaningful Bible phrases; ' God is love,' for instance.

" A revelation of what I always wished rather than a change, though none the less real, absolute, enduring, drastic and joyous.

" Simply to come as the Publican, to rest on God: ' God, be merciful to me, a sinner.' "

He was talking with his mother about this whole experience, and he said something like this:

" When I went down there to work, I told them I was not sure that I was theologically sound. They said that didn't matter at first—and wasn't the end to begin with; if Christianity was worth trying, to try it and see if it worked. I did—and it does! "

IV

IN SPITE OF HIMSELF

THERE used to be at Princeton a boy I really knew only at a distance. I used to see him shuffling along the sidewalks, surrounded by a host of good-natured and not over-intellectual collegiates, singing harmony, telling comical yarns, chewing the stem of a pipe. He was the most relaxed human being anybody could visualize. He was always in for a musical evening, a " bull-session " on athletics, a pleasant evening in New York. Everybody knew him, everybody liked him. He was the best friend most of the rounders had, but he never was a rounder.

He had a reputation for good-nature. I knew about him mostly from his room-mates. They were both class officers and had been touched by the work we were doing. One of them used to talk about him, and of what a delightful person he was, what a cheerful soul when he waked up in the morning, what a joy to live with. But he had come from a very religious family, and while he was in college he was taking a spiritual vacation. We never saw him at anything religious. He gave me a very wide berth.

43

He graduated, went into business, got engaged, and married happily.

About that time his younger brother was a senior in college. He was the idol of the family, and one of the most widely beloved boys I ever knew. People smiled when you spoke of him. Strolling into the building one day, he and I fell into conversation. Then we had another. One night in early spring this lad gave his life to Christ. It was a decision which took everything with it; for he decided on the ministry, as well as on the Christian life.

This decision produced a reverberation in his older brother, and a sense of possible misgiving. But nothing came of it until a couple of years after, when he and his wife began to feel the lack of something in their lives. They were happy— amazingly and uninterruptedly so. His business was going well. His wife had been an exceptionally popular débutante, and together they were asked everywhere and had a wonderful time going. They thought maybe they needed more religion, so they began to look about for a church. They tried a good many churches which their friends attended. They came down to us. At first they were a bit critical, and seemed not to understand what we were aiming at. But finally they decided it was as good a place to take up regular attendance as any other; so they handed in their names, and said they wanted to belong; thousands of other young

married people do the same thing—" One simply
has a church one belongs to."

One Sunday after church, as they were going
out of the door, I asked them if they were engaged
for dinner. He made some excuse, but his wife
said that it didn't hold, and they came. We
talked about many things through dinner, and then
adjourned into the study. After a quarter of an
hour his wife got up quietly, went into the drawing-room, took down a book and began to read.
I was feeling a little groggy, after a long morning's work and a heavy dinner, and had no thought
of seeking a serious talk.

But he began. His theme was in general that
we had something he did not have. That was evi-
dent to him. But his life was very full. He was
extremely happy in his marriage, and his business
suited him exactly. He did not feel any sense of
need or any sense of sin.

I explained to him that if he meant by sin tear-
ing around with somebody else's wife, or getting
away with crooked deals in business, or beating his
wife, he did not sin. But it might be sin just to
let the whole center of life be in his office and his
apartment. It might be sin to have nothing else
to give people but good humour and a smile, for
when a man is in deep need these are poor medi-
cine. There were people in the world who had
found a Power which could be transmitted into the
lives of others. That Power was the one solution

to all problems, and without it men go on the rocks. He prided himself on being unselfish. All right—what did he have to give a man who was drinking too much, or driving his family mad with temper, or thinking about suicide? Had he that kind of a Power to give away? Did he know the men right in his own office, down behind the masks, where they really lived?

Next day he called me from his office, and said he knew more about himself than he had the day before. He was seeing things differently.

It happened that the next Sunday the Queen of Rumania was coming to the church, and I thought it would interest our friend to be asked to usher. He liked being thought of, and appeared at the church done up in his best and looking very gorgeous. It gave him a feeling of being included, which was what he needed just then. That afternoon we went to meet Her Majesty, and had an interesting time. At the reception he asked me whether he should come that evening to a service in the church, or join another group where personal religion was going to be discussed. It was a rainy night, and I thought the service would not be particularly inspiring, and urged him to go to the other meeting.

There he met with another group which was trying to live, upon the basis of God's guidance, a life surrendered wholly to Christ. As the meeting came to a close, he wanted to talk to somebody.

He sidled over to P. G.,[1] and said he would like to talk. They found a comfortable sofa, and sat down and spent an hour or more upon the great questions of religious experience. When the ground seemed to be cleared for him, so far as talking without experience can clear it, P. G. suggested a Quiet Time together. So they prayed together, opening their minds to as much of God as he understood, removing first the hindrance of self-will, allowing the Spirit to focus an impression upon the mind, like light upon a camera exposed.

There and then he lifted his own life to God, giving Him entrance and sway. "Now I know what you mean," he said to P. G. For the miracle had happened—the age-old, everlasting miracle of second birth. A man had surrendered, and God had accepted him. The realization came at once, a sense of liberty, of peace, an inward glow and a sense of rightness.

Going home in a taxi, he told the taxi-driver what had just happened to him, with the same gayety and buoyancy which used to go into songs and parties at college. You must know him to get the extraordinary spontaneity and naturalness of all this, the smile of amusement at his own willingness to be open about these matters when the chance presents itself. The elevator boy heard the story as he went upstairs—I suspect with some

[1] Persona Grata, in *More Twice-Born Men.*

surprise that religion " took " highly respectable people in just this way.

He slept for six hours, and then went to the office. He had hardly more than sat down at the desk before another man came up to him and said: " ——————, I have been watching the change in your face for a week. Something has been going on inside you. I wonder whether you can give me any help? " It was a man in desperate need, just such a man as we had thought of together, quite hypothetically, fifteen days before. He said: " Twelve hours ago I could have said nothing to you. But I can say something now."

At the Thursday Evening Group he joined us, and told the story of his change, with more utterly engaging humour and more moving earnestness than it is possible to describe. Laughter, for this crowd, seems to be the best wrapping for that which cannot quite be held out in complete exposure; religion has tried solemnity, and men feared it; sentimentality, and they despised it. Perhaps the religion of this day needs to be mixed with natural and ordinary humour. What dogmatism and gravity and learning and oratory have failed to do, humour may succeed in doing; namely, helping us to let religion run down into the hidden places of our souls till the whole is leavened. Truth seems to get in on a smile which would stay out on a rhetorical effort. The wholesomeness of a life like this is transparent; but there is

something here more than most people ever find—
and that is a *basis* for laughter. He had found
Christ, in an experience. And he was sharing the
gladdest thing that had ever come to him. That
night, as he stood shaking hands with people, you
would have thought he had just announced his en-
gagement! He cabled his brother in England
about his conversion, and had a warm and welcoming answer. A birthday was being celebrated
—a spiritual birthday.

When there is such a vivid sense of being *within* this kind of a fellowship, there is bound to be
also a consciousness, for some, of being *without*.
The bond is between those who have genuinely
found Christ and espoused finally His life for
their own. Anyone can find Him who wills to, so
that the fellowship is extended as, one by one, human souls find their way back to Christ. The
want of depth and vividness of experience is what
has robbed the Church of this element of fellowship which once it had and which it would have
again if enough people were transformed.

His wife had looked on at all this with great
understanding and sympathy. But it was with a
little envy and from a distance. It was great for
her husband, but . . . to have him soaring up
in these spiritual regions was almost like losing
him a little bit.

Some days later I dined with them and their
sister and brother-in-law. They wanted the whole

family to have this experience, especially these two with growing children who were asking questions they had not the conviction to answer. After dinner the girls went off to talk alone and, while trying to talk her sister into the experience, his wife realized that she was trying to give away something that she did not really have. And there and then she accepted Christ for herself.

Together they have begun to do great things for Christ. Although they go to dinners, dances, theatre parties, concerts, with the old crowd, all their social life is permeated with the spirit of deeper human understanding. Spontaneously the subject of religion comes up almost everywhere they go. With absolute naturalness they talk of what has come to them, and of the difference it is making. A beautiful human love has been consecrated to a spiritual coöperation. There is a Third to all their counsels and hopes and plans. Literally their week-ends, their social evenings, all their spare time, is at God's disposal. They touch the lives of young people of the sort whom religion generally does not touch. They have found a wholly new experience in each other, as they have surrendered each other to the will of God for each, and been willing to be used, separately or together, as God wants them to be used.

Human love is a glorious thing to see under any conditions—but human love with God all through it, is heaven.

V

TO DO OR TO ENDURE

A HALF-CONVERTED seeker, pulled towards the world by a thousand small dissipations, and drawn towards Christ with a deep desire to serve Him somewhere in this world of human beings—that was where she was when she turned up one evening at the Thursday meeting. She had heard that there was something happening here, and she came to see if it held anything for her.

She comes of a family of privilege, where religion has been part of the order of the day—an assumption. Civilized people pay respect to government, learning, high office, and deity. Religion goes along with the code of well-bred people. Unhappily that kind of religion does not do very much for those who are earnest and in need.

All her grown-up years she has been a restless, self-willed woman, of tremendous desires and uncontrolled moods. Lavish generosity would alternate with petulant insistence upon her own way, or peevish self-pity when she could not have it. There was force in her, if guided and directed, but it was like that of an engine lying on its back with all the wheels going full speed. One felt in her potentiality for generous and outgoing understanding of human beings, but until this personality was captured for Christ she could do nothing for others.

A few years ago a serious illness brought her up short with some thought of the meaning of living; she felt even that Christ had work for her to do. And she set out and took a job which appeared, on the face of it, to be a place where she could serve Him. A trial at it helped and lifted her for a time, but then the old undisciplined life came back, she slumped into the accustomed self-indulgent ways, and was more discouraged about herself than ever. Fine occupations and good surroundings do not change the hearts of people or give them an experience of God. The people about her took her for granted, because she was engaged in humanitarian and religious activity— and a divided heart was all she had to put into the work.

She came to the Thursday group because she was curious, bored and had nothing else to do.

" I saw something in the faces of the people there, a light and a joy," she now relates. " They were so alive, so thrilled over the stories they were telling. Some spoke of how they had been won for Christ, others of how they were being used by Him to win their friends for Him and His service. The whole atmosphere was so real it made me sit up and take notice. Several people asked questions, and they were answered directly yet kindly. No matter how trivial the question, it had a courteous reply; the group sometimes laughed with a person, never at them. And the atmosphere was gay but with a great earnestness back of it."

There she heard the word " surrender " used a good many times. At first it sounded like putting oneself in chains for life. But it had so evidently made these people happy that it must mean a great and life-giving relationship to God. She wanted to know more about it, for she wanted happiness and peace.

Pride kept her away for some weeks. She was working in a church elsewhere. Why didn't they have enough to give her what she needed? It was humiliating to go to another minister to talk about these things. But finally she came. We talked rather honestly, and she began to see herself as she really was, divided in her loyalty to Christ. She must go to a person to whom she had lied, and make it right; and it would be hard, for she wanted to stand well with him. There were fundamental decisions wrapped up in the choice of putting God's will really first. They staggered her— and inevitably drew her on to make a full surrender. " After a few days' fighting, I did it. That moment I was converted; I knew it, I felt it; it was as if a load had been lifted from me."

She says that after that miracles began to happen in and through her. She had not been fully happy in her surroundings and her work, and had gotten bitter about it all. "The surroundings did not change," she says, "but my attitude did—and all the irksomeness went."

She felt that this was the message and work for her, and that summer she asked me whether we would like to have her for a full-time volunteer; she had been left an income which made her independent, and she wanted to give her life to spreading this message. She came and began work not long after, and she says: "About the second week I knew that I was in this work for life, and then it was that, all over again, I gave my life, my will and all my possessions to Christ." This was no abstract dedication; she has given to me for the work more than half her entire income this year, besides supporting herself wholly from the other half. There are not many people who inherit independence who do not manage to play with it for a year or so, in travel and pleasure; but not so with her—the consecration was a complete one, and it extended to all she had.

After a few months she began to realize that living a surrendered life means honesty clear through, even to going back and digging out small falsehoods in the past and making things absolutely straight. She shared some old dishonesties that had lain covered up in her mind. "Pride and self-love went again into the dust," she says, "but that is where they belong."

An intense nature has its own problems, and one of them is apt to be extreme feelings about other people. She likes, or she dislikes—and either way she is rather emphatic. Quarters are close in this kind of a fellowship, and there was one woman, as dominant as herself, whom she began actively to hate. While the hate lasted, there was neither peace nor spiritual victory. One night she went to Calvary Mission to sing for the men; but this hate stuck in her throat, and she felt the sham of singing hymns of God's love when her own heart was foul with hatred. She had wondered when she heard men say there that Christ delivered them from drink or some other sin, and she comforted herself by believing that actually they must have used their own will-power. But that night she learned something of moral miracles. For she confessed that sin of hate, and went forward for prayer with all the rest of the self-confessed sinners, praying: " Lord, help me as you have helped these men." And, she says: " Jesus Christ took the hate out of my heart; what seemed impossible was made possible, understanding was put in the place of hate. I felt like Pilgrim when his burden fell from his shoulders at the foot of the Cross. My song was shaky, but my heart was glad! " And that hate has never come back.

Many an eager nature is craving a chance for a " warfare glad and grim "—for work which will use up the energy with which God has endowed them, and do great things for other people. The pity is that so many trifle away their time in service which accomplishes so little for others, and which is so mild that it does not take and use all their own strength. But this woman began effective witnessing for Christ in the spirit of a glad crusade.

One Sunday she went for lunch to an Alice Foote MacDougall tea room. Across the table sat a woman her own age. Neither was the kind to make up to strangers by nature, but there was a smile when somebody passed the salt, and one advance led to another. Histories began to be exchanged; the father of one and the husband of the other had been consul in the same Canadian city, many years apart. Both liked music. One was studying it in New York. That led to, " And where are you? " Calvary Church was the answer, and she grinned a broad assent when asked " How she liked it " ; and that evening the Lady Across the Table was in church, interested in so many young people, delighted with the warmth of welcome, thrilled by the music, and generally very much at home. After a few visits on Thursday nights, she made her surrender with the same woman who had met her in the restaurant. It literally changed her from a person with I at the center to one with Christ at the center. Laughingly, at one of the Thursday meetings, she told of how it all had happened. She has gone back to her own city a wonder to her friends and family; there she is forming her "own Thursday Night Group" and winning individuals. One ought not alone to produce Children of the Second Birth, but grandchildren as well—we are never content unless those who are touched touch others and this beneficent process of spiritual mathematics goes on "till the whole is leavened."

"Of all the vital points in this message," she says, "guidance has been the hardest for me to grasp. But I know what the leading of Christ is in my best surrendered moments. At times I have doubted, in a foolish human way, the existence and the power of the Holy Spirit, so of course I could not then get guidance. But later it comes to me powerfully that it is a sin thus to doubt and limit the power of God. I have to surrender the stubbornness of my will many times before I am led. Guidance is very real to me when I am not trying to manage my own life, and when I am putting God's complete will first. Christ has lately been giving me guidance in a most marvellous way."

It has fallen to the lot of this woman to suffer a great deal of pain in the past few months. Sometimes she is able to be about, but has to be relaxed and willing to rest when needful and not to overdo; for an enthusiastic nature nothing is harder than that kind of restraint, and nowhere does genuine spiritual consecration and discipline show itself more surely than here. At other times she must give up altogether, and be content to lie still. Such occasions are the testing-times, when we find out how much we really believe in prayer as a force, in the love of God in suffering and idleness, in the witness not of lips only, but of life. In her own room, great decisions have been made, and great renunciations which grew out of saying to God: " Nevertheless, not my will but Thine."

But steadily we have watched a deepening sense of the presence of Christ, a more thoughtful companionableness with those about her, the impact of her own consecration upon others which brought life to them, and the sure and growing subjection of all things to the will of Christ. The impetuous force which used to be, like Simon Peter's, all waywardness and caprice is giving way to the stuff which makes apostolic personality, strong and sustained in the redemptive passion. Her life is the growing answer to the prayer of a hymn to the Holy Spirit:

> Breathe on me, Breath of God,
>   Until my heart is pure,
> Until with Thee I will one will,
>   To do or to endure.

VI

GOING IT TOGETHER

YOU may see in the congregation, on a Sunday, a very noticeable little couple. You have a sense of their happiness in being together and of their satisfaction with life. Something irrepressible and laughing seems to bear witness to a great inner joy. At Thursday Group meetings one or other of them is apt to make a real contribution, and after the meetings you will usually find them talking with earnestness and gayety to someone whose face shows need. Their story shows how finding God together has meant also finding the fullness of life.

One of his first recollections is of having taken part in a Sunday School contest on the life of Christ. There were 150 questions, and whoever answered the most of them correctly got the prize. This boy memorized the answers to all 150 of them, and won. So far as he was concerned, it might as well have been about Hannibal or Napoleon—it was just a chance to win a prize. God and Christ meant nothing to him personally.

His mother cared very much about her church, and her religion was very real to her, but her talks with her boy left religion somewhat misty in his mind.

It was not until he was engaged to be married that he began to take a serious interest in religion. There never had been a time when God was not real to the girl. She says that she had not always acted, or even tried to act, as God wanted her to, but she always knew that He was there. Because of her faith, and his love for her, her husband wanted to go with her in her religion; but he came at religion from the rational angle—while her attitude was that there were certain things you felt and knew, and that was the end of it. They might have intellectual sanction, but her experience was real, and that was enough for her.

In school he had had the good fortune to make friends amongst some fine boys, and in his early youth he was kept from the grosser sides of life. Then he was in the army during the war, and there he began to meet sin in its stark forms. He managed to keep clean, although he was " ragged " from morning till night by the other men. He says frankly that he was afraid of the consequences of the kind of life they were living.

But there was a residue from this experience. Certain pictures had printed themselves on his mind, and he could not forget them. After he got home, there was a terrific struggle with vile thoughts, and all that they involve. He truly loved the girl who was to be his wife, and he made a valiant fight, but he never felt that he had won a completely satisfactory victory.

He found that the reasonable way to investigate religion was to consider what it has done, and is doing, in other lives. Some time before his marriage he went to a conference where twenty fellows of his own age were sitting about talking very naturally of their experience of God. He listened, angry at first, then disturbed, then interested, then hungry for what they had. One of the men told him of having been through just such a struggle as his own, and of finding victory through Christ.

Our friend said: " Bill, the trouble with me is that I can't find a personal God."

Then Bill put to him the most astounding and arousing question he had ever had asked: " How have you looked? " " I realized," he says, " that I never had really looked at all. I was interested in finding out about God, but not in finding *Him*."

He tried it, experimentally. He wanted to see if it would work even for one week-end. He didn't sleep much that night for thinking of all he had to do and to change. He knew he must be honest about himself with the rest of the crowd—and one fellow there just idolized him! But he went through with it. He confessed the sham and need of his life, and says that when he finished, he " had a curious feeling of lightness, as if a great burden had been lifted off my shoulders." Before the week-end was over, he had made the greatest de-

cision of his life, to surrender himself uncondi-
tionally and for always to the will of God.

The adjustments which he had to make were
hard. There were days when he let his Quiet Time
slip, and he was making only tentative efforts to
win others. One day we had at the Rectory a
group gathering to which he came—and from
which he went away to his office, where, beside his
desk, he made a fresh consecration of himself to
more active living for Christ.

A few months later they were married, and
started to live jointly according to God's will. It is
something over a year ago now, and he says, "We're
still working on the same basis. When I realize
the pitfalls into which we might have fallen during that first year, I am conscious that it is the
only real way to live. To have a higher allegiance
to turn to—that is what has meant so much.
We're both convinced it is *the* way to live."

Some men find God through Christ, and some
men find Christ through God. He belonged to the
latter group. Some time after the initial experience, he began to look into what had happened to
him, and he found that Christ had little place in
it. Yet he heard others of us talking much about
Christ. He did not yet know who was the Re-
vealer of the salvation he had begun to find. One
night he heard a sermon on " The Personal Christ "
which, in his own language, " hit him between
the eyes." He says: " Next morning, when I got

up to have my Quiet Time, I knew something radical had happened to me. Before my prayer-time was over, I knew what it was; I had found Christ. I had found for myself the power of the Living Christ in my life. I suppose there are other people who, like myself, have found God but have not found the Living Christ. I believe we should not rest content until we have helped them find Him." He and his wife are busy working with individuals. "People are hungry for what Christ has to offer," they say. "We have been brought into touch with a number of them. All like to hear stories of changed lives. Some have themselves made the great decision."

He says that people ask him how all this works in business. "The answer is very simple. If God's will is for me to be in business, He also has a way for me to carry on my business. I believe it is His plan for me to stay in business unless I get definite orders to go elsewhere. I work better, get more done, and have a clearer perspective, than ever before in my life. There is no question that the business man individually can do God's will and stay in business."

He says that it has not always been clear sailing, and that there are times when he gets discouraged and blue about himself. But invariably it is because he is somewhere temporarily unsurrendered. "But I can say I have never seriously considered giving up my original decision for surrender. Life on any other basis is inconceivable, no matter how difficult following Christ may seem at the moment."

This is the way a girl, with an instinctive but unvital religion, has come to a genuine experience; and a man, with a doubt and a need, has had both satisfied in discovering Christ. Narrow means have not kept these young people from the realest of all possible wealth, or from the spiritual health and glow which is the reward of the single-hearted. Together they build the foundation of a home upon the surest of all ground—common devotion to a common ideal. " Each for the other and both for Christ," is the way she puts it. Professor Hocking [1] has described this basis for married life in a great sentence: " The only being you can love is a being who has an independent object of worship, and who holds you out of your self-indulgence to a worship of that same object." Small fear that such a home will split and go to pieces; for it is founded upon a rock.

" I don't know all the future holds," he says. " But God knows. And He'll tell me in due time. That's the great thing about being in tune with His will—you don't know what's coming, but you know it will be the best thing, if you are perfectly ready and willing for it. That ' certain uncertainty ' is what makes a great life! "

[1] *Human Nature and Its Remaking,* W. E. Hocking, p. 363.

VII

A FOOL FOR CHRIST

SHE came to me with a ready-made plan to organize the young people of the parish. She was doing organization work over all the diocese, and thought we ought to have such a society in our church. It was still early in our experiment, and I remonstrated to the effect that organizations did not come first, but changed lives —and we did not yet have enough of these to leaven a whole group. She was thinking in terms of machinery; she had not yet begun to think in terms of people.

She was the shyest person I have ever seen. There was in her beauty of spirit, and eagerness of mind, and unselfishness enough to change the world. But she was thwarted and repressed. There is a self-effacement which is in fine contrast to the noisy bravado which calls attention to itself so readily in this generation; but this was not self-effacement, it was sheer human crucifixion. I wondered how the spirit struggling within could be liberated to the kind of service it was intended for.

She has written an account of that liberation herself; and I give it in her own words, without quotation marks, for her words are better than mine:

All my life I have felt inferior. I have never thought I could be as good or as useful as the people around me. I felt it at home, in school, in college, travelling in Europe and in several different jobs.

From most points of view, I have no reason for this feeling. I came of what is supposed to be the best stock in America. Father's family have lived in New England since the end of the seventeenth century, and a direct ancestor is a Revolutionary hero that every child knows. Mother's family are old Philadelphia Quakers.

We have a family life such as few families have. We play together a lot, and discuss everything from table-manners to education, from speed-laws to religion. Father and Mother never have had the idea that " children should be seen and not heard." They have discussed everything with us as though we were their equals in experience and knowledge, and given our opinions their full value, and allowed us to make our own decisions. The word " family " means to me long walks, motor-drives, tennis, bridge, and sitting about the fire reading aloud. Sunday was always looked forward to, for Father was at home, and we always did something specially pleasant with him.

Then, too, I have had everything I wanted that

money could buy. We live in a good-sized suburban house, with generous land about it. We have always had lots of animals about, and plenty of chance for sport. I have had a liberal allowance, and have been free to go anywhere I pleased and do what I chose. If birth and ideal surroundings and everything that money could buy and the nicest family in the world were all that were needed for happiness and contentment and fullness of life, those things should have been abundantly mine.

When I was fourteen I went to the Brearley, one of the best schools in New York. The next five years were not easy. I was slow at studies, so I spent lots of time out of school studying, instead of playing with other girls. I tried playing basket-ball and other games, but I was not good at them because of the legacy of a mild attack of infantile paralysis. These things did not make it any easier to make friends with other girls. Also I came from the country and they were city-ites. They did different things, wore different clothes. I remember the agony of wearing high boots when the other girls wore oxfords!

I tried to get even with my inferiority by a swelled head. To cheer myself up I used to remind myself (and sometimes others) that I was " a first family of Boston," and just as good as anybody else. I liked the teachers better than the girls, so I spent my recess talking to them—and then boasted about my popularity with the faculty!

During the last two years of school Mother thought I ought to learn something of the gay life. So I had some dancing lessons and solemnly went to a few parties near home. I had gone to school in New York, and knew very few of the young people, so I sat propped against the wall much of the time. I was tall and conspicuous, and the gentlemen did not flock in my direction.

About this time I began to feel consciously inferior at home. Father is an idealistic and a deeply cultivated man, and I never could produce conversation which was really stimulating to him. Mother is a tremendously competent sort of person, and has always done everything better than I, from running a dinner party and keeping house, to managing a charitable organization. She has always run the family. I never questioned her decisions for my life, except to wish I had character enough to stand up against her when we disagreed, instead of succumbing weakly.

My older brother is a very good-looking, enchantingly attractive boy, and very cultivated. He would have adored having a flapper sister who would have been a credit to him, and brought reams of other flappers to the house who would have amused him . . . or else one who would interest him intellectually. I was neither one. I have generally admired him from afar, and been uncomfortable when we were together. My younger brother and I have at times had a pretty real relationship. He is a theorist, and we have spent hours talking over things. He suffers from a physical handicap which would have downed most people, but has given him an iron will and sometimes a caustic tongue. He has real ability and brains, and I have told him more about myself than almost anyone else. It did not occur to me to tell much about my inward self to Mother— she was busy, and it did not seem to me important enough.

Then came Smith college. I began living off the campus, which was not socially the " thing to do." but in the middle of the year got moved on to it. The girls were very nice to me, and asked me to their rooms. But I did not go. I didn't feel I was really wanted—there would be other girls there whom they did want, and I would be uninteresting. Finally they gave it up in despair, and left me alone. And there was I, longing to be liked, but not knowing how to raise a finger to help matters! The glee club was about the only thing that relieved the situation at all.

After sophomore year, I couldn't bear college any longer, and I begged the family to let me go to Europe with my aunt and uncle. Father thought at first I had better stick it out at college: but the work had gone so miserably badly that he finally consented to my giving it up altogether.

I loved Europe. We travelled slowly, taking time in each place to see everything carefully. It was all new, but I began to love the sculpture and the pictures and the architecture. For the first three months I thought of nothing but the sheer enjoyment of life. We were seeing no people, so I had nothing to fear or feel inferior about. After that I was to go and live with a French family outside Paris. I rather looked forward to being on my own for the first time.

" Maman " was a sensitive, shy person, thoughtful and introspective, and not very happy. She was going through the throes of a religious experience. All her family had been for generations Protestants—and she was undergoing a conversion to Catholicism, after twenty years of rampant atheism and bitterness. I was interested in it all, and began to think for the first time seriously about the why and the whither of life. I came to some rather atheistic and rationalistic conclusions, which could not be squared with the religion of my godmother taught me from babyhood. I was a little excited at being on the " inside " at a regular conversion, and jealous because I could not agree with the things which " Maman " was then thinking. I had never before met real sorrow and bitterness, and hers overwhelmed me. By the time I left, she had come out into clear faith which was making life easier for her, indeed making it nearly triumphant; but she was unable to translate any of it into terms which would help anyone else. I grew to be deeply fond of her. I never suffered as I did when I left her.

All the time I wondered why I could not have that relation to my own mother. I was happier in France than I ever had been at home. The people did not know of my failures back home. I had bought a Ford, which was useful for taking the family out to drive (and contributed to my small supply of superiority). I was taking piano lessons, and my teacher was quite encouraging about my prospects; there was this beautiful relationship with a woman twenty years my senior.

But this content did not last. When I got home, the awful question presented itself, " What are you going to do with yourself? " Mother advised social work, so I took a job in a child-placing agency not far from home. I was glad to have something to do, but I was far from happy. We social workers did not seem to be getting very far with the people we tried to help; and I soon got discouraged with my part, and then cursed myself for want of character and stick-to-it. The old discouragement swept back upon me—I had no more intelligence than before I went to France, no more power to stand up to Mother, no more social ease. I thought the discontent was going on forever.

Let me go back to my earliest memory of religious teaching. I remember as a child going to stay with an older woman I loved and sitting in her lap and hearing her say that God was closer to us than we were to each other. I would hug her with all my strength, and she would add: " Yes, much closer—all round us." She taught me how to be a good Episcopalian. She helped me to grow into a habit of prayer that has never left me even in my doubting times. But I sometimes wish she could have shown me how to apply my religion to my life. She had had a religious experience. Her religion had stuck to her even through the knowledge that, though she wanted them frightfully, she would never have children. A religion that could do that ought to cure inferiority. But somehow I wonder if she has ever let her religion run down into all the nooks and crannies of her life. Why couldn't she make it real to me?

We used to argue about the creed, and the Church, and conduct. But I never learned the connection between the three. I used to refuse to go to see girl friends, saying they would not want to see me; and she would tell me how silly I was, and how shyness was selfishness in its root—and I would go off and curse myself for being selfish, and wonder how in the world you could cure yourself of it, and think that I would give my head if I could find out how not to be shy. She used to tell me to read my Bible every day and go to church; I realized my duty in both directions, but they seemed to do me no good. I was confirmed when I was twelve, and I kept on working in the church for the next ten years. But it seemed to have nothing to do with my inward attitudes or my ordinary life.

When I gave up my job as a social worker, I took another under one of the outstanding men in the Episcopal Church. I took it for no reason at all except that he was a friend of the family's and I assumed anything he was doing was worth while. He proved to be one of the loveliest people imaginable. I think I have never seen the God-Spirit shine out of anyone as it shines out of him. He gave me a huge organization to plan and run. He did not know the details of it himself; but he believed in the people connected with it, and in me, and he thought all would be well. I tackled that job because I loved that dear old man. But at the end of six months I went to him and told him it was not getting very far, and that I wanted to do something which touched people more definitely. Something more like what the apostles did—not just boom a big organization. For I had begun to have a vision of what the Church, Christianity, Christ, could do for men in the world.

I came down to Calvary Church to try to get a young peoples' group organized here. I was told they were not ready for it yet, because only out of transformed lives could there be made such an organization. Then the question was very simply asked me: " Have you ever really given your own life to Christ? " I did not know what it meant.

We talked for two hours about God's plan for the universe, of His plan for individual people, of how you could find that plan and live under the dominance of the Holy Spirit, of how it meant letting go of your own plans and desires for your own life, and trusting that God could run it better than yourself, as He saw fit to use you, not as you saw fit to serve Him. In the act of self-giving we agreed; one had to be willing to break with anything wrong one was doing. I thought of a man to whom I must go with apology, and seek to create a new relationship. It was growing definite.

We talked about the possibility of a religious experience in everybody's life, and the need for sharing it with others. In other words, the point of the Church and Christianity was not just to hold services and run organizations, but to see to it that people were made different because they had some Christian connection, some real hold on Christ—different in their ordinary lives, less selfish, less irritable, more courageous, more radiant, happier.

Here again, as all through my life, inferiority got the better of me. I didn't believe I ever could be good enough for God to use me. I knew I would not be able to get up at crack of dawn every morning and take time for Quiet with God. I knew words would fail me if I tried to tell anybody else about it . . . and so on. This went on for six months. I was still at my job in the church organization. I began to talk about personal re-

ligion, and surrendering one's life—but it did not
sound very convincing.

I began to discover that I was trying to do on a
large scale, in many different localities, what I had
never learned to do in one place. I was telling
others how to do a job I had not learned to do myself. I needed specific training in touching the
lives of individuals. And when I was offered the
chance to come and work at Calvary, I took it.

During the first month, I did not accomplish
very much. I talked with lots of girls, but nothing much seemed to come of it. One day one of
the boys said he had always felt inferior, and now
he was praying that God might give him humility
in place of inferiority. That seemed a good prayer
for me to adopt for myself.

Then I went away for vacation. When I looked
back on my start, I had another attack of spiritual
blues. Other people seemed to be doing so much
more than I was. One Sunday morning I went to
church, and the Epistle was from Corinthians. St.
Paul refers to the fact that he used to be a perse-
cutor and says: " I am not meet to be called an
apostle . . . but by the grace of God *I am what
I am.*" I took that to mean that God made every
one of us just as He meant us to be, with qual-
ities and even limitations which He wanted us to
have and which He wanted to use. If He made
me as I am, presumably He had a job for me in
this world that I could do, a job I would just fit

into. If I were willing not to be a success in *my* way, but simply to do anything *He* wanted me to do, He could and would show me the special job for which I was born into the world.

Next day I was sitting on the roof of one of the sleeping porches of the house, looking out over a glorious sweep of water, towards some blue hills and the sunset beyond them. I was not thinking of anything in particular, just sort of wallowing in the beauty of it all. I was counting those little lighthouses as their lights flashed in the distance, thinking of the hope they hold out, the way men depend on them. They were so out of the way— but for the ships that passed, so necessary.

While there the thought flashed into my mind of the words of the leper to Jesus: " If thou wilt, thou canst make me clean " . . . and I added, " of my inferiority." The words came with a conviction which only those who have felt the guidance of the Holy Spirit can know. As I thought about it, my inferiority was a sin, a dirty, loathsome thing like leprosy. I was no better off than that pathetic beggar, even if I was of a right-hand top-drawer family of Boston. And if I could be cleansed of the inferiority, I should be free from my worst enemy, and then I might be used of God. And if I—a person who had never been really of any use to anybody—could be used by Him, why then any human being could find Him and be used by Him; and I knew that I must tell people that.

*   *   *   *   *   *   *   *

She has been used of God, and most marvellously used. The channel of a personality empty of self is God's great channel.

She met a woman, some years her senior, a conventional Christian who through the death of her mother thought she had lost her faith. She still kept busy with church organizations, and did a great many religious " things," but they gave her no satisfaction, no peace. The " fool for Christ " said that the solution lay in a great surrender to Him. The two women talked for a long time, and then the messenger proposed prayer. " But you don't understand," the woman remonstrated, " I surrendered long ago." The Fool for Christ asked forgiveness, if she had presumed to deny an experience which had already come; but then they did have prayer, and *she* prayed a prayer of self-dedication. After this the older woman prayed herself, aloud—and rose from her knees saying that this was a totally new experience; nothing like it had ever taken place before in her life. And she calls that day the day of her conversion. She, too, has become a witness.

There was a young wife, gay and cheerful without, but carrying a load of unhappiness within. With her husband she came for a meeting, and listened. At first it seemed vague and indefinite, then it grew personal to her. Next day, at another meeting, the married girl flew upstairs in tears, and

straight after her went the Fool for Christ. She
entered into the situation quickly, with amazing
sympathy, they got all the barriers down, and the
whole story out—and then they had a prayer together which was the release of the soul of this
young married woman. Her conversion has involved the conversion of her husband, and her two
children have found an experience of God through
them.

A secretary in a great insurance company office came to church. She came again and again.
In the porch of the church an introduction led to
acquaintance, acquaintance to friendship, friendship to a real talk. She thought that she had made
a decision for Christ, but she found no courage to
speak of Him to anyone. And what must she do?
Together the two new friends went to the Mission
one night, and afterwards they sat over an ice-
cream soda, and finally had prayer together across
the table there. The stenographer did not pray,
only her companion. The stenographer had not
found the Spirit which gives men " utterance,"—
and that was the issue for her, willingness to speak
in Thursday Evening Group, the willingness to
give voice to her faith. Till she should do that,
she felt she was not surrendered. After that
prayer, she won her courage. She spoke in the
meeting. She brought her own sister around, who
has become also a carrier of the message. In a
quiet way she is a very effective messenger.

In a service in another city we met a girl who comes into New York every day. She wanted this experience, but she said she left home too early every morning to keep a Quiet Time. The issue for her lay there, in willingness to make time for God. They agreed that the solution might lie in sitting on the train with one girl instead of four, and keeping their Quiet Time there together. In their bags they carry little paper Testaments, and like John Wesley of old, studying and praying on horseback as he took his way from place to place, they make use of the hour that many people waste.

The Fool for Christ says that it has been interesting to watch in how many cases she has had to deal with people who needed " bucking-up "—just exactly what she had needed, people who felt inadequate or inferior or incapable.

She says that three great convictions have come out of trying to live this kind of life:

The first is that " the lowest worm of a person is important in the eyes of God." That conviction cut down to the roots of her inferiority, and gave to her, not a relative and contrasted importance with reference to other people, but a sense of intrinsic and absolute worth which works in the mind, conscious and subconscious, and drives out the hounding sense of fear and self-depreciation. I myself doubt whether the roots of inferiority can be extracted in any other way.

The second is that for her indecision has been

eliminated by the experience of guidance. Always before she had been tremendously influenced by what other people thought, by the conventionally unselfish or proper thing to do; the last person she talked to could always twist her out of a decision. That is gone. Her life is based, with a daring which is startling, upon the Voice of the Spirit; and in sheer results she is efficient as she has never before been efficient in her life. " The wind bloweth where it listeth . . . and thou canst not tell . . . so is everyone that is born of the Spirit." The surefootedness of a life like this is incomprehensible to one who will not sympathetically study its basis.

And the third she calls a " consciousness of adequacy." She means that if it is right for her to be in a place, she can meet whatever situations may arise. If she is meant to talk to somebody, the words will be given her. If she has to challenge someone in high place to a finer ideal, the power to do so will be present. Nowhere has this confidence more wonderfully shown itself than in her own home. One day, sitting quietly in the living-room with her mother, she said: " Mother, I feel like a person in this house, for the first time in my life." The quality of self-effacement has not been lost by this new adequacy, but rather enhanced and given scope and opportunity. One no longer feels sorry in her presence for the pathos of an imprisoned personality, one feels the glory of the wonder of the presence of the Spirit of God.

VIII

WHERE BROADWAY TURNS

THE Thursday Evening Group is the stamping ground for all sorts of people, the rendezvous of various faiths and nationalities. Here coincidence turns to Providence by the admixture of God-guidance, and chance acquaintances become milestones and turning-points in the destiny of human lives.

One night an acquaintance lingered to meet and talk with a woman some years his senior, who had come for the first time to the meeting. She had been long a Christian, but lacked the joy which was her birthright. As she started for the door, he signalled another woman of about her age, and said: "I think you two might like to know each other." A few words passed between them, pleasantries edging over towards seriousness.

Two days later these two women met together. The newcomer was a quiet, seeking sort of person, who had been bound for years by anxious, unreasoning fears, and religion had never done anything for her, because somehow she did not quite know how to give it the opportunity. As she sat and talked with a sympathetic person, albeit a person who has never known the sensation of fear, the fear which had walled her away from God and her own best self began to blow away. Inner fears and anxieties disappear when brought into the sunlight, as germs do. Presently the two prayed together side by side, to the accompaniment of wholesome laughter from an invisible group across the hall. She surrendered to God her groundless fears, and with them turned over to Him her life for His direction.

The transformation was immediate—and extraordinary. The deep lines smoothed themselves out of her face, and her brooding, tired, almost tragic eyes filled with light; she said: " I am happy."

Later she asserted, somewhat timidly: " This is wonderful for me, but I shall never be able to speak to anyone else of what I have found, the way you all do." Her new friend gaily said that she would never be able to keep still! And so they parted.

One of the rewards of such sharing as had brought these two lives close together is a sense of fellowship, of something so warm and outgoing towards other human beings that, were the word not preëmpted for something more like sentimentality, we could only call it love. This shy, diffident woman had found not only God, but a tremendously increased capacity for profounder human relationships. Unreal religion makes for inhumanity; but real religion brings to the fore every scrap of genuine humanity in any life, every touch of

companionableness and good humour and reciproc-
ity.

A few days later, she was buying some china in
one of New York's great department stores. She
had been there before, but it was when human faces
were not so friendly as they had now become.
The boy who waited on her was an eager lad, in-
telligent, painstaking, and his English accent was
the occasion for a conversation.

He proved to be the son of an English clergyman, a kindly man and wise in many respects; but
he had brought up his son in the ordinary way, so
that he was more intimate with the forms of the
church than with the power which impelled his
father's life. A younger brother had died some
years before, and this young boy heard his father
say from the pulpit that his faith in immortality
was deepened by his loss. The boy listened, out of
his own sorrow, wondering. Would he ever feel as
his father felt? He doubted it.

Then he set out for America to make his way.
And as America walked past the counter where
he sold china, he found it a lonely place. After all,
nothing is so lonely as to be in a great crowd of
people without a friend in it. He was of a little
different quality from the clerks about him, and
this fact distanced him still more than his foreign
origin. Even the great church which he attended
held itself aloof.

" Do you like your church? " asked his customer,

as she gave him her address. "No," he replied,
"where I go I do not feel comfortable—there are
so many silk hats!"

And then, although it was not her church, she
described to him something of what he might expect to find at Calvary. "You'll find all sorts of
head-gear there," she said, "and some come in with
none at all. It is a church where a boy is made to
feel at home, no matter what his clothes are like."

The very next Sunday he resolved to make the
experiment. He came to Calvary. He liked it.
It seemed to him real, he says, and downright and
human. He decided to come again. Our staff of
a dozen young people stand in the porch of the
church for nearly an hour after service, talking to
old friends and making new ones. About his second visit, one of the men met him and asked him
to the Staff House for dinner. There he found a
group of very diverse people, giggling at one moment, talking about God's guidance the next, and
the conversation was all shot through with refer-
ences to something they all seemed to know about,
something which made them very gay and cheerful, and seemed to put a zest for life in them which
no one could miss who saw them.

His host took him off to his own room, and there
they talked. He found out what the "something"
was which bound these extraordinarily different
people into a unity. It was an actual experience of
Christ, in terms anybody could understand, any-

body could experiment with. Conversion, God-
guidance, winning people, Quiet Times—all terms
for something which had always seemed musty to
him, and a little mysterious, though he was fa-
miliar with what they named. The man who
talked with him had been delivered from fearful
sin and fear, and he shared himself confidently and
without self-consciousness.

The young Englishman made his decision. He
gave himself to this wonderful Christ.

He began to come to the Thursday Evening
Group meetings, and there one night he told us
briefly and pungently of his experience and his decision. It is quite impossible to describe the radia-
tion of spiritual gladness which is thrown off into
the atmosphere of a room when a man or woman
for the first time stands up to witness for the Lord
Jesus Christ. There comes a quiet elation into the
hearts of those who understand, which is a kind of
this-world counterpart of the " joy in the presence
of the angels of God over one sinner that re-
penteth." How this melts down boundaries the
world erects, jumping over differences of age, race,
colour, creed, and every natural predilection, is one
of the amazing results and rewards of this life.

A little later he fell in, at church, with a young
physician who has been attending here most of
the winter. The spark of friendship jumped
quickly, the physician saw something in this boy
which he needed and wanted, and they agreed to

have dinner together some evening. And there
they talked, until the physician declared his willingness to have done with compromise, and to serve
Christ with all his heart. So quickly is a field
turned into a force; a man who needs to be urged
towards a decision one week is urging decision upon
another the next. So grows the number of witnesses
for Christ. So run the fires of the Spirit, setting
alight life after life.

One night the English boy spoke longingly of
England in the spring. "I thought of going over
and getting a job in the country for the summer,"
he said, "but I cannot bear to leave Calvary."
And as he was leaving the Thursday meeting one
evening, he said to me: "Do you know that the
interest of all this has eclipsed every other interest I have? I think about it all the time. It
has become the center of my whole life."

William James said that religion is either a dull
habit or an acute fever. What a gorgeous experience it is when religion becomes " the center of my
whole life " !

IX

IN A STEAMSHIP OFFICE

THE average minister is likely to persuade people to continue to do something they have never really begun, or to excel in doing something which they have never decisively contracted to do at all. He is telling them how to round difficult corners, and get a second wind, in a journey towards which they have never yet crossed the starter's line. Into the regions of spiritual aspiration the people may follow him with their imaginations; but generally he has failed to reckon with those sullen and stubborn rebellions which lie at the bottom of men's hearts, the congenital trust in things which can be felt, the obdurate unbelief that any practical man can take the Sermon on the Mount seriously in twentieth-century economics, the disposition of almost all men to consider what we hear from a pulpit as deserving to be taken with a grain of salt, the plain practical divorce which the ordinary individual makes between the occasional flight of his imagination Godward, and his common every-day life manward. The average person in the pews has never been told how to make Christian experience a fact instead of an aspiration. Many so-called Christian people have never definitely, in any clear-cut and decisive way, begun their Christian life.

The ecclesiastic may say that I am impugning the validity of membership in a church—that here is where the believer's life in Christ begins. But I do not believe that a person can break into the Christian life without a step vastly more radical than merely joining a church now ordinarily signifies. I do not believe you can make such a mild entrance upon a warfare like the Christian life. You can accept the creeds that way, you can get used to church services, learn a lot of pious things by heart, and adopt those little conventionalities by which we confine our worship to such a *very* decent and *very* orderly procedure.

But no man becomes a Christian merely by getting used to the feel of it in others. It cannot be done without the old inward " consent " of the personal will; and in this day consent must mean something much more starchy and stringent than mere acquiescence. We want something decisive, which cuts us away from the old life, and from the rest who are content to live it; we must dare to come out and be separate. We seem to have lost the power to obtain from people a ready and rugged and all-comprehensive self-dedication.

That is what church membership ought to mean; what it does mean is generally nothing more inspiring than becoming another pew-filler. The state of the Church at the present time, its place of low esteem in the mind of the outsider, its impotence in the affairs of the world, its level of complacent contentment with a little round of pious duties, is witness enough that we are in an age of decline—for all our fuss about money and fine organizations—an age of spiritual powerlessness and decline. It is time that somebody dared to be alarmed. Church leaders are dangerously near those eminent obstructionists in the New Testament who "entered not in themselves, and them that would enter in, they hindered." Something is desperately wrong with the thing we are doing for and with our church people; and it is my contention that the trouble goes back to the very start, or rather to the want of any conclusive start at all.

The story which follows seems to me terrible proof of this thesis. It is the story of a woman now nearing middle age, the daughter of a clergyman.

If anyone had told her before last summer that she was not a Christian, she would have been very much surprised and greatly indignant. She was doing, and had long been doing, things which she knew were decidedly wrong—but except at certain times (which were growing more and more infrequent) her conscience did not particularly bother her. Other people, she felt, were doing far worse things than she, and yet they seemed to flourish. She had plenty of friends, and was much respected.

She grew up in the shadow of the Church, and with a great love of the services. She sang in the choir, and taught for years in various Sunday Schools; but it was all without any real sense of a personal Saviour. When she read her Bible, it became only a kind of textbook, so she gave up the reading. She did not really pray, though assiduously she " said her prayers."

" I went to church at least twice a Sunday," she says. " It was a habit. I was really miserable whenever I had to miss a service; yet why this was true I do not know. The music, the poetry of the psalms, the sermons, good, bad and indifferent, all seemed to have their place in keeping me loyal to the Church.

" But what good was all this Church-loyalty to me in every-day life? As I look back on it now, I see that it did not keep me from being dishonest in thought, speech or action; it did not keep me from falsehood and making a good story out of a few facts; it did not keep me from telling yarns that were ' off colour ' when occasion arose. It did not draw me close to my family, or keep me from losing my temper, or saying sharp things and hurting people's feelings. I was not an easy person to get along with, at home or in business."

Her friends wondered what was the matter with the Church that she could not get help there. But she had not accepted Christ with the Church, and did not have Him in her heart. Church was to her a formal observance of religious rules—little more. She would not have acknowledged it, but she was practically " without God in the world."

" If anyone had pinned me down as to what good I was getting out of my religion, I could not have told them; nor could I have helped anyone else with the simplest problem in their life—though I had a great many theories about what was right for other people. I was a fine combination of Pharisee and hypocrite.

" I was discouraged, and sick of myself. I masked all this by trying to be chipper and gay. A game of bridge takes your mind off yourself—and the theatre, and being in a gay group of people. Some of my friends said they knew of no one who seemed to enjoy life more than I."

One Sunday in the early summer she came down to Calvary Church. She had heard about a group that was meeting to study the life of Christ in His dealing with individuals. It sounded interesting, so she came.

At the very first meeting something began to happen to her. Some of these people had something which she lacked. We were studying that amazing fourth chapter of St. John's Gospel, and Christ's dealing with the Woman of Samaria. A thunderstorm was raging outside, I remember, but the air was electric within as well as without. For the first time this woman began to see there might be a way out for her from her troubles. She went home counting the hours till the next week.

She brought along two girls to the next meeting, and they heard strange things, about the Holy Spirit really speaking to people to-day, about God working miracles through individuals, and she suddenly realized that that meant something actual, and was meant for her.

She began to pray and have a daily Quiet Time. The Thursday Evening meetings she looked forward to as " lights in a dark world "—for this was all uncharted sea for her. Not that she was very comfortable when she got to the meetings, she says, with a load of unconfessed sin on her heart pulling her down. Her spirit was a battle-field where neither side had the upper hand. " I did not know what to do," she states. " My pride held me from going to anyone in the group. I thought it would be traitorous to my own heritage if I should look for an upheaval in my spiritual life."

Then she noticed in the papers that on a Sunday in August the subject of the morning's sermon was to be " Do Church People Need Conversion? " She made up her mind she would hear that sermon. And during the Holy Communion which followed, she gave herself without reservation to Christ, determined that she would let Him guide and use her life, no matter what the cost. " And here we offer and present unto Thee, O Lord, our selves, our souls and bodies, to be a reasonable, holy, and living sacrifice unto Thee."

And this took place, not in a rescue mission, not at a revival meeting, but in church, and after she had said many times that her church did not believe in conversion!

About the middle of the following week I had a talk with this woman. I asked her how things had gone at the office. " Ripping," she said, and told me of something that had happened that day. One of the men on another floor came down to borrow her scissors, which she had just bought new to cut clippings with. Next day he was to bring them back; in their place he came with an old pair of dog-toothed scissors that would not cut through butter, saying, " Won't these do just as well? " She astonished him by saying, " Oh, yes, I guess they will! " To which he replied: " In heaven's name, what's come over you! " And then she told him.

That day she said that she wished to make a thank-offering to be used for the extension of the same kind of the work which had meant so much to her; she had no money, and nothing of value but her late mother's diamond ring—and she wished me to take that and sell it and use the proceeds for the work. The value here was far greater than money; but sentiment, memory and every other value went into this great offering.

Now, conversion sometimes has a way of working backward, and demanding to include in its sweep and scope old and almost forgotten situations. It has been said that to give up sin men must do four things: Hate, Forsake, Confess, Restore.

About seven days after the experience of conversion, I had a letter in which this friend said, " After three hours of absolute *hell* I am beginning a letter, and I hope God will give me strength to finish it. In a few sentences I'll have to tell you something that has been in my mind for years. Your opinion of me will be changed. It's the kind of thing you would expect to hear from a member of the Down-and-Out-Club, not from me. I am shamed and humiliated, but it will have to come out. While I worked for the ————— I stole money from the institutions. Not much, it is true, but that does not matter. I could never have confessed this before Sunday. I need help badly to go through with this thing, but I'll carry on."

Then came the temptation to send a money-order and so, as the Chinese say, " save face." But guidance was clear; she must send it back in full, with interest, and sign the letter with her own name. There may be shallow people who will call this squeamish; but the real reason why most people who have slipped into wrongs like this do not go to the logic of absolute honesty, is that they lack the courage and thoroughgoingness of this brave and consecrated woman. And because they are easier on themselves, they never know the clean sense of being right with God, with no barriers whatever. It is not surprising that a few weeks later, on vacation she wrote: "I feel like singing all the time now—Te Deums, etc. I have not said *much* to my friends yet, as I am waiting to have a little more guidance. I can truly say I have never been so happy."

In about three months came this letter: "So many things have come to me within the past three months. Things I would have done as a matter of course before, I turn away from with utter disgust. Of course I still have my daily struggles, and need to be continually on the watch, guarding my lips, temper, etc. But even with my failures, I am not discouraged—that is one of the many wonderful things my new scale of values has showed me. You may be interested to know that my work is to be changed. Mr. G. called me into his office last Saturday and said that they had been 'watching me these past three or four months,' and had decided to give me a much more responsible position. I was so overcome that I hardly realized till afterwards that this might have been an 'opportunity.' The things I used to worry about now amount to nothing. I take absolutely no credit to myself for my changed attitude towards my work, and towards the people with whom I work."

There was an old longstanding problem of misunderstanding with her father, which sooner or later must be healed. We often talked of the best way to help this clergyman to understand what had happened to her, without hurting his feelings and making him feel that he had failed his own daughter, who had failed him many times.

Her next vacation she planned to spend at home, and said she hoped for " great things to happen." There was a little too much of the idea in her mind of " making him to see things my way." She had guidance that the best thing she could do would be to " live her religion." The night before her return she sat at her window for a long time, feeling that she had not done as much as she should. A few days after she got back, however, she received a letter from home containing this sentence: " I never enjoyed having you home so much."

This little woman has brought many people to us in trouble, and helped many to see what happens when a conventional Christian finds Christ. Her testimonies at Calvary Mission are simple and direct, and sometimes the word of a good woman can do for destitute men what no other word can do. I used to feel about her that she was tied up in the mechanics of religion, interested in the outwardnesses, working about the church but missing the core of the matter; I feel that no longer. Nor does anyone else who comes into contact with her. There is more humanity, more enthusiasm, yes, more personality.

Here are some of her convictions about keeping a daily Quiet Time along with God, the first thing in the morning:

" When I find myself getting formal in prayer, I find it helps to pray out loud; and this helps me also when my mind tends to wander. I tend to pray with petition when I am on my knees, and so I generally sit up when I want to meditate or listen. It was a great shock to my ecclesiastical conventionality to find one did not have to kneel to pray to God! But I am glad I learned it.

" I find that reading Moffatt's Translation of the New Testament, after I have read the passage in the King James Version, is a great help to understanding it, especially in the Epistles. I recall my extreme prejudice against any translation except my beloved King James, not considering that the desire of God must be that I know the sense of the passage as well as enjoying the vehicle of it.

" Quiet Times do not need to be confined to morning and evening. One of the most profitable Quiet Times I ever had was one Saturday afternoon on the top of a Fifth Avenue bus. The traffic swirled about us, but amid that confusion and noise God spoke to me as surely as ever He had at home or in the stillness of a church. I often stop in at Trinity Church, downtown, for a Quiet Time at noon, when things have gotten a bit on my nerves at the office. The early morning is the *best* time for Quiet, but not the *only* time.

" I believe definitely that God speaks to people directly through the Holy Spirit. When I began to listen, I think I had the attitude of a child who expects something to fall into his lap off a Christmas tree. I wanted guidance tied up and labelled, ' Guidance.' I made the mistake of thinking so hard on certain definite matters about which I wanted guidance, and wanted it quickly, that it became a strain instead of a relaxing, so naturally nothing happened. Nobody can force God's hand. There are times when He says nothing, and only wants to impart the sense of His presence and concern. I get a great deal of my guidance on my way to work, or during a church service.

" Sometimes you do not find out till afterwards that guidance is genuine. You act on it, and nothing seems to happen. God works at both ends of the line, with you and with the other person He wants you to win; and we need to be prepared for a quick victory or for a long siege. He may give either.

" Have I ever regretted the cost of my decision to go the whole way for Christ? I can honestly say that I never have. I have regretted the sins which pulled me down from time to time since I made it.

" But what a relief it is to know that God can and does forgive, and can use you in spite of everything! Thank God that, though my eyes were first opened to the picture of what I was—a

Church Pharisee,—they were also soon opened to what I could do for Christ by His help."

She has made, she says, blunders when working with people, but which of us hasn't? She has given one person advice which she knew that person wanted to hear, rather than run the risk of hurting her with the truth. She has sometimes "kept back part of the price," rather than lose the good opinion of a friend. She has sometimes been silent when she should have spoken, so she says. But she thanks God for other times when she has been truly a messenger of God.

Things in the office and at the house are very different. Her whole sense of values seemed changed. She is becoming more and more able to take things in a quiet and calm fashion when once they would have made her "hit the ceiling."

The interest you can take in people who were once uninteresting or whom you once disliked, is a wonderful thing. I suppose it comes out of the fact that more and more we discover that we are all alike under the skin, all in need of the same thing,—a personal loyalty and love for the Lord Jesus Christ.

X

RELEASE

ONE is brought into contact with people sometimes through strange and symbolic means.

A few Sundays after I had come to the church there was a Communion Service. And, in accordance with a long-time custom of the parish, I invited all to come to that service who loved the Lord Jesus Christ and were trying honestly to follow Him. I believe we need not apply artificial and man-made safeguards to protect this great gift of Christ to the world; it protects itself by its own purity and power, and men will not go to it unless in their hearts they feel drawn to it; and if they feel drawn to come and receive His help, I know no better criterion than this to admit them. If some of them do not quite understand the holy and solemn significance of this great act of worship on our part, and this extension of His life to us on Christ's part, I think they are more likely to find out by experiment than by telling them they sha'n't come.

That day there came to the rail, for the Communion, one of the men responsible for the music. He was in his vestments. He was not of our branch of the Church, and he had not been long amongst us, and was not accustomed to our ways. I gave the cup into his hands, and he thought that I should keep hold of it—and for a moment it tilted, and some of the wine was spilled on his white cotta.

I thought that he would be feeling badly about this, and so I made a point of seeing him after the service. With that graciousness which is a part of the sensitive nature of this man, he told me at once how badly he felt about it, how unhappy an occurrence it had been, and how sorry he was for it. I simply said to him that no one was really to be considered but the Lord Jesus Christ, and I could not imagine His being offended by a mistake. Instead of this incident being unrelieved misfortune, God turned it to use. Again the outpoured wine became part of God's redemptive plan.

For as we walked arm-in-arm down the aisle of the church, my friend said that some day he would like to have a talk; some things were troubling him, and he would like to thrash them out. We agreed on the following Wednesday, for lunch together. It turned out to be a scorching hot day. After lunch, we made our way back to the old Rectory. In a cool, closed room we talked. And this was the gist of his story; he tells it himself:

"When I think over my life I am strongly impressed by its lack of coördination; by the suppression of most of its worthy ambitions and de-

sires; by its want of unified purpose. I have felt defeated, and in recent years a kind of apathy has settled down on me in consequence of it.

" This defeat has come because I have professed religion and have not lived it. I have accepted its general teachings as being true, but not its transforming power within.

" The first recollection of my early home brings back an atmosphere heavily charged with religion. My father, who is a minister, and my mother have always had a consuming devotion to religion and church work which has left little or no room for any other interests, save the life of us children, our schooling and social life, and the community enterprises in which we were all of us bound to have part."

One of his earliest recollections had to do with family worship, which came as regularly as getting up and going to bed. The doubts and waning spiritual interest which have come in recent years have never been able to destroy the reality of those early family devotions. They have stayed in his memory, and been always a kind of beacon.

Another definite recollection brings back an experience in the Colorado town where he lived as a boy. The family had all gone to hear an evangelist in a near-by church. When they returned home, an elder brother, who was twelve or thirteen, was in great distress. He and his father talked alone. After a time the family were called for worship,

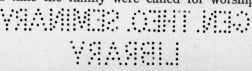

and his father explained what conversion meant, and then they all prayed. It was plain, when this brother prayed, that this new experience had come into his life. The old lingo was gone. There was an original grasp on religion in this boy, young as he was. His few broken sentences had in them the ring of conviction and personal self-surrender. This fact moved the younger brother very much. But he said to himself right there that *he* could never make such a display of his emotions. This decision to keep all his religious feelings to himself grew more set as he became older, and extended to all his other emotional experiences.

One wants to pause here long enough to say a word about emotion and religion. I suppose that it is very well to be on one's guard about the giving of free rein to emotion, and I can only remember four times in my life when I have been deeply and rousingly moved by religious emotion. But, in the fear that emotion shall seem to register a reality which is not present, do we not forget that, as J. M. Robertson [1] says, " There is no process of reasoning which fails in its throb of emotion in the exact degree of its depth and clearness " ? Or, as Benjamin Kidd [2] says, " It is the control of emotion, not the absence of it, which is the mark of high civilization. Other things being equal, the higher and more complete the individual or the

[1] *Essays on Ethics,* p. 188.
[2] *The Science of Power,* p. 124.

people, the higher and more complete the capacity for emotion." I think we could well dispense with some of our characteristically modern self-consciousness about emotion, and face with commonsense the fact that it is not the element of naked rationality which moves men to live greatly and for high ends, but rather the element of concern. The urge of power is the capacity to care.

This man felt the all-consuming fire of his parents' religion which made them very sensitive to wrong in others, so that to do something wrong and displeasing to them would not only cut him off from their confidence but would also bring great pain to them. Consequently, his code of morals became a matter of pleasing them. Religion for him was doing what they wanted him to do. And so naturally religion began to seem like a constant source of limitation, a cramping and confining of himself. It was a question of serving man who looketh on the outward appearance, instead of God who looketh on the heart. It was a matter of code and precept, rather than intention and desire.

I believe that most conscientious Christian parents would deny that this situation exists in the training of their own children. Yet I am sure that, in many cases, this is where the matter stands.

Now he has come to agree with these early standards in the majority of questions, but it was not until he was able to determine them for himself.

" When I was sixteen," he tells us, " I left home
for a long tour of the country. I played the piano,
and travelled for nine months. When I returned
home it was with a keen desire to be a fine mu-
sician. My family had moved to a great city. The
boys of the neighbourhood were more developed
than I, or at least more grown-up. They went as
they pleased to dances, theatres, and parties.
They thought only of amusement and girls. Just
as my religious instincts had been bottled up so
far, now I felt that intense interest in music was
a thing which could not be shared with the boys
and girls whom I knew.

" As was said of Charles Lamb at school, ' while
others were all afire and play, I stole along with all
the self-concentration of a young monk.' "

It was not until he was nineteen that he went to
a great city and established his own mode of living. He made a few friends, studied intensely, and
yet wondered why he was so dissatisfied with life.
A love affair went on the rocks, and this com-
pleted his misery. A change had to be made.
After days of work and nights of agony and sleep-
lessness, he decided to enter a profession.

The fraternity question soon arose after he got
to college. Five young men had started out twenty
years before to found a fraternity which should be
characterized by clean living, good scholarship, a
democratic spirit, and participation in the worth-
while activities of the university. From the first

this organization was a success. Swearing and in-
decent stories, even dancing and smoking, were for-
bidden in the house. Almost all the men were from
Christian homes. Some were embryo ministers.
Others were solid, stalwart country lads, with little desire at first to enter into the whirl of a large
co-educational institution.

"But during my college days a great change
took place," he relates. "Some of the younger
alumni thought we were wrong, to try to be different from other fraternities—prudish, hypocritical. We started a petition to be admitted as a
chapter of a well-known national fraternity. We
held smokers for our guests. To overcome our
feeling of social inferiority, we tried in every way
to be just like the other fraternities. And we soon
achieved our aim. I can think now of thirteen men
during my college generation who planned to enter
the ministry; only two have finally landed where
they said they were going. God has a plan for
every life—and when a man dodges it, something
dies in him. Nothing adequate happened to dis-
suade those men from their first purpose; it came
from a slump in morale, pure and simple. Who
can estimate the loss of idealism and spiritual
power in the other sixty or seventy members of
that fraternity during my generation in college?

"College left me in the air. Music had been
most successful. I did not know whether to enter
the ministry or go into music. I thought I should

compromise—on church music. So I went to New
York to continue study for a couple of years. I
resolved that if I felt a strong urge towards the
ministry after giving music a real chance, I would
change over. Music took every minute of my time.
When a man is busy he is supposed to be happy,
but the old fits of depression kept coming back. I
still seemed divided and inwardly uneasy. Something was still being stifled within me. I was unhappy. And sometimes I seemed useless."

I seem to remember the brilliant philosophic
summary of *The Gentleman with a Duster* that
we need " the Greek element in our minds, the Puritan element in our characters, and the Christian
element in our souls." I think it a very profound
judgment upon the best elements in our moral
discoveries through history. The subject of this
sketch is in love with beauty, and has been for
years; and with a widely awake and appreciative
mind, I think he may be fairly said to have
achieved the Greek element in this sense. It is to
me heartening to know that there are many homes,
especially through the western part of this broad
land, where the best elements of Puritanism are
found still to obtain; I have watched the sons of
households like that, in schools and colleges, for
some years past, and they are generally the back-
bone of the institutions where they go. Puritanism
after all is only a form of that restrained and reasonable asceticism, plus a Christian sanction behind

it, which every man needs to practice if he expects to be disciplined at all.

But the Greek element easily slips into dry rationalism or antinomian worship of beauty. And the Puritan element readily becomes stiffness and legalism and harshness. The two have often been found at enmity with one another, a thesis against an antithesis. We need a synthesis to fuse the two. And " the Christian element in our souls " is the synthesis. I take this Christian element to mean a kind of grace of humour which is fundamentally a sense of proportion, a gentleness which is both strong and firm, a strenuousness which is soft-hearted, a certain willingness to sit loose to life which yet does not smack of compromise, a certain power to see the other side of things which yet does not topple us off our base, that something which comes to a man who has learned to look outside of himself for his final sanctions and standards. It is the thing which the real saints have something that holds opposites in equilibrium, till life becomes at once a poise and a harmony. This our friend lacked when we left him at the close of the last paragraph. And this is his own account of what followed during our talk:

" In a few minutes I had told my new friend of my dissatisfaction with life, my unfulfilled desires. I saw that religion might become so absorbing as to be almost violently attractive. And I knew that I needed more of that kind of religion.

He told me of the moral and personal reservations he had made in his own earlier life, and the great change which had come when he voluntarily surrendered these in order to follow Christ. In a few minutes my troubles had been simplified and resolved themselves into the need for one small but momentous act—the giving up of every vestige of personal ambition, or my own plans for the future, and then going to God to ask Him if He would take charge. I was willing to try this New Way. In that old empty room—become suddenly full of significance for me—we knelt down to pray. I had prayed countless times before with other people; yet this time I hardly knew what to say. The old lingo of stilted and conventional prayers did not belong here, would not go here. But I tried to let my heart do the talking this time, and to ' commit my way unto Him ' that He might guide the whole future, and have utter and absolute charge of my life. When we finished, I got up feeling light-hearted and free, for the first time.

" It seems to me that one must surrender," he wrote ten days after his conversion, " all over again every day. I am trying to keep the peace of mind I felt after talking with you that day, and to make it permanent. I am having the most worth-while visit at home I ever had. I think it has been my feeling of independence which has separated me from my family on former visits. To conquer that is my biggest battle now."

Later he talked with three of his friends about giving God a chance. One of them, whom he had been after for a long time, seemed more hopeful than ever before. One of them wants to go to work for Christ at once.

In his old church in Chicago he was able to talk to the Young Men's Club about the vital experience he had had, and to speak with one or two individuals. For the first time he could tell them in an enthusiastic way of a religion they come to church to find, but really refused to accept and to live.

In the autumn he returned to his music in New York. He has been promised a great future in it by those competent to judge. But there are two great loves in his life—music and religion. In the one he is assured a place of success, leadership, remuneration. In the other, he steps into something almost unknown, so far as his own leadership is concerned. Slowly the issue has had to be drawn between the two. The quick judgment of the world would be to take the line of least resistance and assured capacity, and stay in music. But there is an objective side to be considered, too. Does the world need music to-day quite as much as it needs religion? Just take one unit of honest man-power, where is that unit most needed? For the position of a man like this in music there will be a dozen applicants, scrambling to have it. For the position in the ministry, there may be none.

One day he came in to talk, sorely torn between

Then we got to his family. He told me all the unhappy situation which has been described. I have seldom seen in a youngster such a mingled attitude of outraged disappointment in his family, and the tenderest, gentlest, yearning and loving desire to stand by them and see them find a new kind of life. He told me that he wanted to love them, that in his heart he did love them. And he wanted to live with them. But . . .

Finally we came to himself. I said that for him to have anything with which to remedy the situation at home, it was necessary that he have it first in his own life. This led into his own personal problems; and we talked naturally and openly about them. I believe that we all need to live what my friend Erdman Harris calls " a greenhouse life," such that anyone can look through from all sides, and see what is growing there—weeds and all. This does not mean that we tell everything we know about ourselves to everyone we meet: but that we be *willing* to share anything, holding ourselves ready wherever it will help another. As it is true that sorrow can best sympathize with sorrow, so it is true that sin (or one who has known it, and we all have) can best understand sin, enabling another to make a clean breast of it, and begin in earnest the warfare against it.

Having gotten the matter into the open, dealing with it not as a curse to be kept shut up in the dark, but as a problem to be faced in the light, we could go on to the positive side of the matter. It seems to me as fatal to begin with the solution as for a doctor to begin with a cure instead of with a diagnosis. You have got to find out what you are dealing with; or you will be giving chicken-pox remedies for cancer diseases. Ordinary religious work does not take time for thorough and accurate diagnosis, and therefore is very general, and a little hazy when it comes to cures. Christ is the cure. But how men shall be brought to understand the meaning of Christ, what doors you will open in the man's mind for the Christ to make His entrance through, is a matter which requires on your part the utmost care, an exquisite sympathy, and a deep sensitiveness to the guiding of the Spirit of God.

Somewhere in the course of a conversation like this—maybe before you get at the question of sin, and maybe afterwards—you may find it helpful to tell people the story of someone a good deal like themselves, preferably someone you know yourself, who has had a vital experience, who has collided with a Christ-filled personality, gotten sin into the open, made the great surrender, stuck by it, and is now winning others. A picture will do more than an argument. Drummond said we do not have to prove things to people, but only need to let people see things. This is the thing which gets hooks into the man's imagination, and rouses him to see concretely what religion would mean if it came into his own life. I told this lad such a story, in some detail, and covering in the story itself a few of the obvious kind of objections.

Here I will let him again go on with his own story: " Then came the big question. Was I willing to give up everything for Christ, to live a life as much like Christ as possible? I wasn't satisfied with everything that I was doing. I hated the sight of my brother, and had no liking for my father—though I would do anything in the world for my mother; it is the human part of a fellow to feel that way towards his mother. At first I said I would like to straighten things out with my brother and father. He said, ' Wouldn't it be better to accept Christ first, and then go home with Him in your life, and tell your brother about it? ' He was right.

" I was still for a long time. Neither of us said anything. It was not an uncomfortable wait, a great deal was going on in my mind. At first I said no, but my heart and all my insides were crying yes. I was given a long time to think things over."

At the conclusion of that luminous silence, this boy looked towards me and said what I think was a very remarkable thing: " All right—let's bow to it." It was as though he had said, with eloquence, that all his life the overarching presence of the All-Holy had followed him, the merciful tracking-down of the Hound of Heaven, till at last he

must yield, and submit himself to the tremendous-
ness of that divine Love.

And as he spoke, the tears started from his eyes,
carrying away in their tiny but powerful flood a
mass of old unhappiness and blackness, just as
clean rain washes a dirty street. Those were not
tears of sadness, but of new joy; symbols of the
emotion of moving out of false life into true, out
of staleness and evil and wrong relationships into
a new dawn of one's spirit. Then, if ever, a man
is safe in losing control of himself—when he sur-
renders control to God.

When he had finished, I suggested that we go
down on our knees and ask God very simply for
His forgiveness and blessing. And we did, each of
us forgetful of the other, save as we met before
the Father who hears. This is his own account of
it: " Through my tears I said yes. That was my
only way out of it. We both went down on our
knees and gave our lives to Christ. We were quiet
a while before we got up. I sat down where I
was before. I could not speak. Somehow I was
relieved, free, as though a great load was off my
heart. Jesus Christ was suffering for my sins. I
would go out to do His work, and live by His will
myself."

We talked for a little on the way to keep the
New Life. We talked of the daily Quiet Time, of
Bible study, prayer and listening, and of the power
of God to lead and guide those who are obedient

enough to be led. We talked also of the need for early sharing of the experience through which he had passed, and bringing others to the same place. " When I went out," he writes, " he gave me a book on prayer, how to pray.[1] I have used it much, and will still need it, as it helps me a great deal. When I got out of the house I was a different fellow. I felt different. It was past 11 o'clock. I went to see my younger brother, but was too late to see him that night. I was looking for somebody to tell what had happened to me. On my way home I passed the poolroom where I used to be found every night almost. I felt I had conquered its power over me. That night before going to bed I read a little of the book on prayer, then I had a prayer. The first time in my life, I prayed with a meaning to it, and thanked God."

That was a Monday. On Thursday night I was having a confirmation class. That night this boy not only came, but brought with him two members of his family who had never paid much attention to religion in recent years. Some church-Pharisee was anything but welcoming that night as they came in—as though forgetful that the Lord had said that He came not to call the righteous but sinners to repentance. I thought Christ wanted them there, no matter what they had been heretofore.

---

[1] *How to Find Reality in Your Morning Devotions*, by D. W. Carruthers. To be obtained from Fleming H. Revell Company, New York.

The boy had brought them—and I knew that back of their coming was his own heroic witness where it is hard to witness, right amongst his own.

The next week I was sitting alone, just finishing dinner. The bell rang. In came our friend with his younger brother, whom he introduced in these words, " I want the kid to have what I got." I coaxed them to have a little coffee, and then we pushed into the study. They were both due that night at the news-stand; in fifteen minutes " the kid " must be off downtown for a new supply of papers, and his brother back at the stand. Guidance came strongly that the new lad should go with me to the Mission. I suggested it to him, and asked him if he believed in God's guidance. " Yes," he said, " I do. God often guides me, in a pinch."

It is strange how the elemental and self-reliant who forge their own way against odds know this immediate working of God; and the civilized, sophisticated and comfortable, set round with luxury and ease on all sides, find reasons to reject it, relying either on the infallibility of their own intellects, or those more unheroic promptings of conscience which come to the spiritually mediocre and uninspired.

We listened together for direction. Then I asked them what had come to them. The younger lad said, " I am going to the Mission with you." The older said, " My guidance is, let the kid do what he wants, and I'll handle the papers some-how." The Marathon runner set off at full tilt for his stand.

That evening at the Mission when the oppor-tunity was given for men to come forward who wanted prayer, " the kid " went down with tears in his eyes. He knelt down, and I beside him. He said, " I want to pray, but I don't know what to say." Then he and I together said very quietly, " Lord, be merciful to me a sinner." We went back to the Avenue after the meeting; and the big brother, who had been praying, took me by the arm and said, " Did the kid get anything? "

The next night was a Wednesday. A little group of younger men were meeting at my house, who had been coming together all year to talk about personal religion. They knew each other well, bet-ter than most brothers know one another. I asked our runner to come and join us. He could not come until after the supper was nearly over—and it was not easy for a strange boy to come late into this group of entirely new fellows. But one of them, peculiarly gifted with the grace of tact, said, " ———, I hear you run the Marathon." Our friend's face brightened, and in a few moments he was telling to them much of what he had told to me, and the whole crowd listened well. In fif-teen minutes he belonged to us, and we to him. He was wholly incorporated into the group, and has been one of us ever since.

Soon he grew uneasy about living away from home as he had been doing. He felt that if what he had was real, it could help him curb his temper. And so one night, when we were talking he said, " I think I'll go home. If there's no room, I'll sleep under the sink, but I am going home. And I want to make every member of my family a force for Christ." So he gave up his room on the West Side, and went home.

Things were up and down. Some days went well, others went badly. You could almost tell by his expression when he came in, how matters stood at home.

On the Wednesday of Holy Week, I had guidance to go to the house. It was a drenching rainy afternoon. As I lowered the umbrella, the mother stepped out to meet me, and said she had been praying I would come, " The boy has been so bad." I listened and heard her through, and then turned the tables a little, and asked what help they were giving him with his new life, saying that it was hard to live a Christian life amidst wrangling and fussing—what were they doing to make it easier for him? But I knew, too, that the boy was somewhere at fault. That evening he came to see me, very crestfallen. " I can't stick it at home no more," he said.

But finally the story came out. As they sat round the table after supper the night before, something that had been said enraged him, and by way of an adequate gesture, he took hold of the corner of the table-cloth, yanked it with all his might, and so flung all the dishes into the corner against the radiator!

It did not take the boy long to see that there were better ways to witness for Christ at home than breaking up the crockery—he came to that conclusion quite " on his own." The question then was what to do next. He was very glum, and very serious. Light broke when he said he knew he must apologize for it, and would go and do it.

That night he and his father had the best talk they had ever had, and it began with his own confession. It is strange what a power comes with the self-humiliation of abject honesty and ungrudging apology. They talked away into the night. Next day was Good Friday; and that night, for the first time, he got his father to go to the Mission.

I shall never forget the Communion Service on Easter morning. The boy had been confirmed in March, and signed his inward surrender with outward acceptance of Christ through the church. On Easter Day both parents came with him to the service. Neither of them, I fancy, knew very much of what the Communion meant. But when their son started forward to receive, they came straight along behind him. There was very little theology in their minds—but they knew that boy had found something they wanted. And when he went forward to receive something more from his new-found Master, they came and knelt with him. I never felt surer of the welcome of the Lord Jesus extended to any worshipper than to these two seekers at the rail. It said volumes of the real inner desires of their hearts. And it said volumes, too, of the witness this lad was living at home—spite of a few smashed dishes now and then.

" Next came the time," the boy goes on, " when I first told my story to a group of fellows. One of them told me to come up to his church one evening, he wanted me to see somebody. I thought there was one person to talk to. I found a bunch of them, twenty-five or thirty, and I was the speaker of the evening! It took every inch of nerve I had to tell those fellows what had happened to me, but once I started I worked my way through to a finish. Then I took a little bunch of them aside. And later I talked with two of them individually. Speaking to that group gave me a new desire to see and help other people."

About this time I met again in New York a boy at a great preparatory school, a lad with every privilege anyone could have, connected with a great ecclesiastical family known throughout the country. I thought the newsboy would do him good. So I brought them together. " We were alone in a room," is our hero's account of it, " and were talking about different things, finally got round to this kind of personal work. I told him about myself and expressed myself openly. When the subject was switched round to him, the same results followed. He spoke openly about himself and of conditions at the school where he was. He was interested. After a while he said, ' You are a great fellow, and you would be a wonderful help up at our school.' To that I answered, ' I can't go up to your school, as I must work, but I can go there all the same.' He looked at me in a peculiar way, then I finished, ' What I got, I will give you, and in that way I will go up there.' It was not long after that that he gave his life to Christ, to do the will of God.

" This talk, and bringing him through, brought me closer to that fellow than my own brother. I had only known him for two hours. When he left he gave me his address, and I gave him mine. We promised to write often and keep track of each other. We are still writing, telling of our experiences to each other in this work, with the hope that we may help one another to work better."

One evening our pacer came to the group of boys " to get into the spirit." He was going off to see one of the members of the church, a man twelve years his senior, a man of every opportunity in life, who had attended a famous school and university. This man had been to the Mission one night, and came in afterwards and said to me, " You fellows have got something that I haven't got." Said I, " Do you want it? " " Yes," he

said, " I think I do. How can I get it? " I told
him it was contagious, and I would send him somebody who had a serious case. " Whom will you
send? " I said, " I will send you an ex-newsboy."
So they had agreed to meet.

The boy writes that he " attended the first
fifteen minutes of the meeting. I told the boys
what I was going to do, and they encouraged me
and said to ' go about it slowly, and make what
you mean understood.' I left on my way to see
him. The appointment was at a College Club.
When I arrived he was already there. We went
up to the large sitting-room and selected a corner where we would be by ourselves. After
talking for a while, I said, ' Is there anything in
this world that you are working for that is so dear
to you that you could not give it up? ' I got an
undecided answer. For he realized, knowing what
my object was, that if he said, ' Yes,' I could work
fast, and there would not be much of a way out
for him.

" I told him of other people's experiences and
of my own. We talked for two hours, and then I
said, ' Leave me out of the picture; this choice is
between you and Christ.' He said he had faced it
before and had not gone through with it. Finally
this man said, ' I will try it to-night. Before I go
to bed I will try to give myself to Christ. I will
see how it works.' "

I wish that I could convey to you the mingled

gaiety and gravity of this lad as he had set out for
this interview—his perfect freedom from pride in
his new life and the doors it was opening into finer
associations, his intense prayer and earnestness
that this older man should be won for Christ. And
I should like to have peered in a window at this
ex-newsboy, this young East Side athlete, laying
siege to a graduate of an exclusive school in the
lounge of a College Club in New York!

Hardly anybody, no matter how soundly converted he is, escapes a period of letdown and lapse
at some time. We call it being " off." The old
life claims payment on our mortgage, reaches up
out of the past and lays a dead hand on us; we
get into the grip of the physical; sloth and im-
purity and self-centeredness come back; we get
critical of the people who showed us the new life
and did most to help us find it; we ridicule guidance, we blame others for lifting us so high up
when we have of ourselves neglected the practices
which would keep us there. And our friend was
no stranger to this common experience.

About three months after his conversion, he
failed to come around for two or three weeks. We
missed him. We prayed for him. Some of us
looked him up, and found him friendly but silent.
It was as though the air had gone out of his tires.
He was flat. In place of the ordinary eagerness of
his expression was something lack-lustre instead.
We let him know we were there when he wanted

us—but force him, we would not. He must fight
it out alone. Sometimes he came to the meetings,
but was negative and gave nothing. Instead of
pulling more than his own weight, he was a drag.
This is a time for patience, for thoughtfulness,
some day perhaps for a sharp, earnest, loving word
that goes to the root like a knife that lances the
carbuncle. Once the flow begins, the lapse is
over.

The first sign I had that things were right again
was a month later. Another lad had gone with
him to camp, and gotten into trouble, and left.
While there they had had lots of talk together, and
he had felt this other boy was not living up
to the profession he had made of Christ. As he
started for the city again, the guidance came
strongly and urgently that he go with him. And
so, taking a day out of his own vacation, and taking money out of his own pocket, he took the same
train, and they both turned up at my house. I
asked the other boy to explain what had happened,
and got a garbled tale. Then I asked him whether
thus-and-so was what he saw happen. " I would
rather speak to you alone about this," he said. I
was engaged at that time, and he agreed to come
back in the afternoon. I was forced to keep him
waiting for half an hour in the hall. And I found
that during all that while he had been crying like
a child over this other boy. When he came in
and sat down on the sofa, he told me the straight

story, still talking through his tears, angry with himself for giving way: " I hate to go on like this. I never cried yet over getting hit in the face, or anything like that. But when I give myself to a fellow like I have to him, the best I've got, and then he comes down here, and doesn't play you square on what happened, I am so disappointed in him, I just can't help crying." As with Peter at the denial, there are times when tears are not the sign of weakness but of spiritual concern. It stirred me mightily to search my own soul whether I ever cared enough to spend time and money and tear out my own heart this way for the sake of another man. Later this other boy came in, made a clean breast of it with fine honesty, and our friend took the night train back to the lakeside. " Love never faileth."

In the autumn he was asked to go and speak to a group of young people in Princeton which included some undergraduates. One had come who heard that a newsboy was going to talk about religion; he had no special interest in religion, but this piqued his curiosity. He went. The newsboy spoke. After the meeting they got together and talked, and the undergraduate made up his mind to surrender to Christ. His own comment was: " You can laugh off these big fellows that come down and preach in chapel on Sunday mornings; but you can't laugh that kid off—he's got something." That undergraduate has not only decided for Christ, but for the ministry, and the whole experience came through the newsboy.

What the future holds for this boy, we do not know. I asked him once what he thought about it himself, and he said, " Once I got a flash to get an education and go into the ministry. But it has not come again. I think we'll have to wait." I said to him that some stones were better polished, and some were better rough—and I did not know which he was. He replied that he did not know either, but whichever it was he was perfectly happy. He wanted to do God's will for Him, and nothing else. I never knew a greater surrender than this lad's willingness to forego the possible rewards which might come through some of his new friends and associates, and to be content with doing his own job well, however obscure the world might consider it. We shall wait for further light on God's complete will. Where that Will is, there is always a way. Where He guides, He provides.

Meanwhile he goes on with his work, looking up to God for his direction, looking out towards men for his opportunity. All his impulses for sport and game are loosed in this absorbing activity, all his fight and energy in this thrilling and eternal warfare. Religion, far from cramping, has freed him, and all his powers are atingle when spiritually he is in high gear. Men misname who call this coördination of the whole self in high action by the name of emotion, though there is

given to proving his points in family discussions with pretty sure effectiveness. She lived a busy, active, a happy childhood; was good at outdoor sports; loved to read in her father's library.

She got her first impression of genuine religion from a clergyman who was the father of one of her friends. His sympathy and understanding and kindliness reflected the spirit of Christ, and she loved him. But the ideal which he showed her seemed to her so high that she felt it would mean giving up all the worldly things she loved to do; and for that she was not prepared. She saw the sun glistening on the far fields of the country of holiness, but the road thither was hidden or only faintly marked. She did not know the way.

After her father's death she spent the rest of her girlhood in a boarding-school on the Hudson. The next years were darker. There was an unhappy marriage, and later the need to earn her own living. She turned a fine voice to account, and sang in recitals and church choirs. She tried consciously to get closer to God, whom she knew only in a vague and uncertain way—but no one told her how to do it. He remained unreal and unreachable; and she remained restless and inwardly starved.

A nervous breakdown from which she recovered slowly made life more difficult, and she became the somewhat bitter and cynical person whom I first came to know. She covered up her real self, and blinded herself to her real problems, by her natural gaiety and humour. Taste and style and a crisp conversation can fool the world for a good while. But beneath it was dissatisfaction and the overlaid emptiness of a drum.

She saw about her many nominal Christians, and she felt that a God who was represented by them, and by the cold churches to which she was accustomed, was unworthy of worship. The heart not only knoweth its own bitterness, but takes it out in laying the blame everywhere but on itself. She tried to do what was right, but prayer did not come with church-going, and she says there was no reality in her religion. Through all the activity of a life full of pleasure and excitement ran the consciousness of a desperate need which was at times so bitter as to be almost unendurable. Her second marriage was a happy one, and brought with it a measure of peace. But the vital urge to find something in life worth living for and working for with her whole strength—that was her deepest longing.

One night she came to the group. She saw in the faces of some of the people there the sort of happiness she had always longed for; they were people who shine, who give off rays of warmth and inner harmony and strength. With characteristic energy and enthusiasm, she set out to find it for herself.

All alone, in the quiet of her room one night, scarcely realizing all that was involved in it, she surrendered to God. A terrible restlessness had been tossing in her soul; she lay there thinking rebellious and mutinous thoughts, and then she said to herself, " I've tried my way and haven't found happiness. Why not try God's way? " She did it there and then. And through the hours till morning she lay bathed in a wonderful Presence, filled with unutterable peace and calm. A little while afterwards, on a Thursday night, she told of this experience. Her witness is always marked by the spontaneous humour which has been hers, alternating with deep feeling. She began gaily to tell her friends what had happened. A man she was dancing with, whom she had known for years, asked her: " What makes you look so radiantly happy? " And with a twinkle she replied: " I've got religion! " Then they were off on one of those wonderful evenings in which, in the midst of shallow surroundings, people plumb the depths, and talk about the things that matter most.

Wherever she goes, at lunch parties, at tea, buying in the shops, talking with the butcher, she carries the old air of gaiety, but to it something has been added—something which makes people wonder what has come over her, and wish for more of it themselves. She never " drags religion in," but she finds people " always want to talk about it." To the joy of life—sometimes a bravely pretended joy only—she has added the deeper joy of God; and who is not eager to find the secret of that kind of joy?

" Since that night of my surrender, I have come nearer to God," she says, " sometimes with swift, joyful steps, sometimes slowly and painfully; but I know Him and I love Him, and I feel a singing in my heart that tells me it is well between Him and me."

She has always been a minstrel, a laughing wanderer through the world, giving pleasure to others no matter how heavy the heart might be within; now she is turned pilgrim, and still she goes through the world spreading contagious joy. But it is the joy of a traveller, not a wanderer—a traveller who has found the entrance to the road that leads to those sun-lit fields in the country of holiness where the Good Shepherd feeds His sheep.

XVI

THE ENGLISHMAN

H E had come " out " to America laden with letters of introduction. And hearing that we were by way of transferring our habitat without warning, he thought it wise to look in the telephone book to verify his addresses. Mine was one of the few in New York that matched his envelopes. So early in his sojourn I had a ring from him. He had a letter from a British author known to us both, and couldn't I come for dinner one night?

At the appointed hour I appeared at his hotel, and was greeted by a tall, square-jawed young Britisher of about twenty-five summers. His accent was rather exaggeratedly English, and so was his point of view. We sat down to as English a dinner in a New York hotel as could be found anywhere in London—cold meat pie, boiled potatoes, salad swimming in vinegar, and fruit compote to be taken with spoon *and* fork. Everything but vegetable marrow!

Afterwards we retreated to the roof, for it was in the dead of summer, and there, looking down upon the river and the lights, we talked of many things—of books and travel and poetry and philos-

ophy and men and events. He had been here but
a few days, so differences in custom struck him
more forcibly than they would do later, and he was
not afraid to comment on them. It is said to be
the Englishman's peculiar privilege to criticize, and
our friend made full use of it. We were incurably
materialistic, hopelessly uneducated, and madly
youthful in our viewpoint. I confess he was a difficult Britisher at first. I was torn between scorn
for his insularity and sweeping criticisms, and a
feeling that there was something very fine-grained
and substantial in the real heart of the man.

From our friend in England he had learned a
little of the work which we were trying to do.
This was classified as " evangelical." I spoke to
him a little about it, and invited him to come down
of a Thursday evening to our group for personal
religion. I thought I could see the mane of the
British lion stand on end at some of the things he
might hear, but it might as well be risked. He said
he would come.

That night there were a great many new people.
You cannot get very far in a group whose members know nothing about one another, and I
thought it was time we had a general introduction
all round the group—it is a great leveller of walls
between people, it gets people to show their hand,
and it makes for atmosphere. So we went round
the circle, with laughter and good nature, telling
who we were and why we came and what we were

looking for. Now and then something personal
would come out which articulated a common need.
It chanced that quite a few of those present were
church-workers, and said so. When we came to
the Englishman, in a violently and almost unintel-
ligibly English accent, he ripped out: " This is all
very embarrassing . . . I don't know why I
am here . . . I hate church-workers. . . ."
He then went on to tell of graduating from Cambridge and being out here on business. It had not
been a very gracious performance, and we were all
quite conscious of it. But I had distinctly the impression that this was really no index of the man
himself. People are often critical of others who
seem happy because they are unhappy themselves.
They resent joy in others when they have not found
it themselves. They lay it to all kinds of secondary
causes, but one of the things, I find, which en-
rages many people with this sort of religion is the
incurable gaiety of it. It is not that they want us
grave; it is that they have a pain in their own
hearts.

As our friend went out, he apologized lamely
for his rudeness, and nervously admitted the meeting was " interesting." Something gentle, almost
wistful, came into his face when he spoke of " so
many people talking naturally about Christ."

Next Thursday he was back. And the next.
And the next. He has not missed one Thursday
since. That first evening he had seemed in no

mood to invite him back, but something in the joyousness of the crowd, he admitted afterwards, drew him.

One Thursday night he was sitting on the floor. Some very real things were said that night, and one of the group who had sat near him told me to be sensitive to him, for he looked desperately unhappy.

Saturday afternoon the leading came clearly to me to get in touch with him. In an hour he was in my drawing-room, and we were in the middle of things spiritual. He told me much of his early and home life. His father is a retired physician who is deeply interested in religion and spends much time reading theology and doing lay-reading in a little church. Religion has always been the climate of his life. Yet no one ever took thought for the son's own relationship to God and Christ. He talked privately with two clergymen in London: one gave him a book and one gave him nothing. " It is extraordinary," he added, " that they do not get at a fellow's real problems. I suppose I have *really* been interested in this sort of thing for a long time. But none of them ever helped me to find it out."

A few years ago, he tried the ways of the world, and cut loose for a bit. But it did not bring him any real satisfaction, and he quit it. Settling down to business in London, he lived with a sister—but he had been terribly thoughtless and selfish. We talked of some of the intellectual problems of re-

ligion, and weighed the issue of Christ in his life.
Traditional religion, university education, business
life in a great metropolis and the companionship
of interesting people brought to this man no se-
curity, no settledness, no real discovery of truth
to live by, no real peace.

A week after, I asked him down for dinner. So
sure was he that this was to prove an evening of
great importance that he had a " tub " and put on
evening dress. Said he: " I should have dressed
to go and meet a girl. To-night I thought I might
meet God, so I got ready for Him, too."

That night he did meet God. We talked about
definite surrender of the will to Christ, with all
that it involved. Something was holding him back.
Fear—self—love of ease—breaking with the values
and standards of the past. It is an heroic uproot-
ing which is required, and no wise man takes that
step lightly. Ten, twenty, fifty years hence that
decision will still hold. Let a man count the cost.
Finally with force he said, " I will," and we knelt
in prayer.

No emotion came. Not the slightest flicker.
He had looked for something momentous, a great
enlightenment, an opening of the heavens, a vision.
None came. But in the silence he had given his
life to God. He wondered if it could have been a
genuine surrender, for he felt no sudden and mysterious peace. We talked long about it, and dug
deep to see whether he were withholding some-

thing. But he was not. He had honestly given God everything.

Then it must be that God did not mean him to experience any emotion. The gift of himself to God was all. He had mapped out the kind of experience he expected to have, but God did not see fit to deal with him in that way. One sees very rational and cool-headed people go through a blinding experience of conversion sometimes: and one also sees high-spirited and easily moved people go through an experience that seems as matter-of-fact as the signing of a contract. There is no predicting the ways of God with any soul until that soul comes to Him stripped of everything; then He will deal as is best, according to need and nature.

I urged him to make a practice of early morning Quiet Times, getting alone with God before the day begins its round. And we talked of sharing Christ with others.

He is a busy man, in charge of a large manufacturing plant. No man does a longer day's work than he—nor, I suspect, a more efficient one. And yet I know of no business man who gives the time to working with individuals that this man gives. He can always make time to talk with anyone in need.

Let me tell of one man he has touched.

Some little time ago I called on two sisters, saints in the parish, who have devoted years of loving service to Christ. I asked after the son of one of

them, whose name is still on the record but whom
we have never seen. They gave me his address,
told me of his home in the suburbs, said that his
children went to Sunday School but he never went
to church. It might have been the story of a thousand others. He had been a choir-boy twenty
years ago, and drifted off. Seemingly there was
nothing to hold him. They showed me his picture, and when I left them I asked them to pray
that we should meet.

What was my astonishment when, two weeks
later, utterly without any word from any of us,
the Englishman brought this man into the Thursday night group, introduced him by his name, and
told me he used to be a choir-boy in this very
church!

They had met in a morning dip in the hotel
swimming-pool. Splashing about together they had
gotten into conversation. The Englishman brought
matters round, mentioned the church, and the man
told him of having come here in years gone by.
The Englishman told of the change that had come
into his own life, the difference it was making, the
glorious joy and freedom and power of the Christ-
life. This man came to seek that same Power for
himself. Next week he brought his wife.

Coincidence? That is what the world calls it.
Providence is what we call it—God—the Power
that makes for righteousness, the Love that seeks
us through all our ways, tracks us down through

joy and sorrow, through peace and pain. There are too many occurrences like this to call it just coincidence. The world is full of people, if we could only mass them together where they would show, who have staked their lives on it that life does not go by blind chance, but that it is ordered. It would be hard to convince pray-er, agent, or acted-upon, in this case, that chance ruled the outcome of this extraordinary little drama in a vast city.

Almost all his hours outside business the Englishman is giving himself untiringly to touching individuals for Christ. There is about him such a wealth of sheer animal spirits, such abounding and infectious cheerfulness, that none can come near him without realizing the presence of some unseen Force—for this gaiety is not self-made nor self-sustained. It is derived. He does not turn it on with a crank—it results when he thanks God for the wonder of His mercy.

The change came through a group of people seeking to find and live Christ. All the spade-work was done in the group. There his deepest conviction developed and crystallized. It was not an atmosphere I should have chosen as best fitted to convince a graduate of Cambridge University, critical to the tips of his fingers, of the power of Christ. But perhaps we make too much of human and superficial distinctions. They mean very little to God. So it is that He takes the foolish things of the world to confound the wise. . . .

XVII

THY WILL BE DONE

HE has been surrounded always with every privilege,—of money, education, social position, and personal charm. His father is a scientist of reputation, a wit and in the best sense a man of the world. His mother is a woman of the rarest grace and loveliness. In any community they would be at the top without effort.

After attending one of the great preparatory schools of the country, he entered Princeton. He was a good student, a good athlete, a capable editor on the college daily. But most of all, he was cut out for a college success; there was about him that indefinable something which draws other men of distinction to one, and which means moving at ease in the upper set. But sure popularity amongst the superior cliques involves an occasional slight to the inferior ones; and, being sought of many, he was a snob to some. He took an easy way through college, drinking at times more than he should, keeping to the code by which undergraduates mould their lives, enjoying himself.

In Junior year a religious movement on the campus had greatly interested some of his closest friends. They had come near enough to investi-

175

gate, some near enough to be converted. In a quiet way, religion began to take hold of him, also. He thought more about it. He wondered in his heart about the rightness of some of the things that he did. But too much religion would disturb the smooth course of things, he thought, and he kept a moderate course.

One day he came in to see me, of his own will, saying that he wanted to talk about the ministry. He felt an urge pushing him towards it, but still he was not sure. I told him of what I had experienced in the ministry, of the joy and difficulty and reward of it. It was March of his Senior year, and there were a hundred others like him in his class, debating what to do with their lives. I said no more to him than to suggest that, if he were sure, he should not delay to make up his mind about the ministry and, if that were his call, to tell some of his friends about it, for I thought there were many of them who might be compelled to think of the ministry for themselves if they knew that he were going to be a minister. His own conscience was busily at work; there was no occasion to put pressure on him of any kind.

And then occurred something difficult to describe, difficult to explain to those who see only the outsides of things. He went straight to the room of one of the younger men on the faculty, whom we all knew, and told him that I was driving him into the ministry. The professor took the next train to New York, and came to my room with hot resentment, and told me that I was putting undue pressure on this boy. It is not hard to see that I had happened to incarnate for this young man an issue; I had happened to bring up from without the conviction that his conscience was bringing up from within—and he blamed me for a conscience which was telling him to do something which he only wanted to do with half of his mind; the other half of him kicked against it violently.

From then on he avoided me deliberately. I did not see him; he did not write.

Somebody once said that St. Paul had always produced either a riot or a revival wherever he went; so does all vital religion. And sometimes it produces a little of both. The movement on the campus transformed lives, but it also stung consciences, and a good many were inclined to confuse the inner voice with the outer reminder. The result was a good deal of criticism, and to this our friend added all of his share. He said some *very* harsh things.

That autumn he went to law school. And there he did well. It was hard work, but there was much compensation in the thought of intellectual superiority. He tackled the work with an added vigour because the fact that he was there at all was a continuous inward protest against the possibility that he might have been at a theological school.

The following June he came into his room one

evening, and found a two-paged article lying on his room-mate's desk, the burden of which was that no man could be honest with God about what to do with his life until he was ready and willing to do *anything*, to be shown, to surrender to God's will. In the silence of his study, that article focussed and sharpened all the issues which had been gathering in his mind all the fifteen months before. He said it might have been written to him as a personal letter. He went into his room, knelt by his bed, and gave his life in surrender to God. He got up, wrote a letter to his mother, and then a letter to me. It was the bravest letter I ever had; it ended, " Please forgive me for being the cad I have been."

During the course of the summer in Europe which followed, he prayed long one night for light on the matter of his life-work. There came something very near to a real vision, and with it the conviction that the ministry was his work. He wrote me a letter, saying he was going into the ministry—and then sent a cable saying he was not. He engaged rooms at the theological seminary, but he also kept his rooms at law school. He says that uncertainty of decision has dogged him ever since he was a boy, and that he never heard the Biblical description of Reuben without thinking it was meant for him, " Unstable as water, thou shalt not excel."

When he got back from abroad, he wanted to

see me. He was still in a fog. The ministry—or
the law? He had done well at the law. On the
other hand, the leading had come in prayer for the
ministry, and the work there did seem more important. There were forty-eight hours till seminary opened. I told him I would not put an ounce
of weight on any side; I would tell him what I felt
were the relative needs of the two fields, and their
opportunities. He must make his own decision
on his knees.

In two days he was at the seminary. In two
months he had met his fiancée, become engaged to
her, and discovered that even preparation for the
ministry may be engrossingly fascinating business.
He felt that if any " signs " were wanted, they had
been provided.

It was towards the end of his last year in seminary that I took over the work at Calvary, and he
was one of the men I most wanted to help me
tackle what we all knew was a very difficult problem in reviving an old church in a depopulated
neighbourhood. By this time he was married, and
comfortably settled in an apartment far more attractive than he could have had in New York. All
the human urge was to remain where he was, and
he made one human decision to stay there. But it
was hardly made before he knew it was wrong, and
he and his wife agreed to come to New York, because he felt within him the deep call of God that
this was where he was wanted. It took another

surrender of self to root up pleasant associations, and change a happy work for one which was uncertain and surely more difficult. I was then out of the country, but he cabled me he would come.

Through the eighteen months which followed our beginning, he kept at his work with great faithfulness. He was untiring about calling, about dealing with situations of human distress. He was growing in intellectual understanding of what constitutes a message. Everyone loved him. Outwardly it was such a ministry as any young man might be proud to call his first work in the church.

But something was lacking. Something inside himself. For a period of time, he would seem fairly to shine with " the light that never was on sea or land "—and then he would slip back into methodical and dogged hack-work. He talked with people, but they came to no conclusions. There was sweetness, sympathy, good sense—but there was not power, there was not genuine inspiration. Now and then came a flash of it; he spoke well at a Mission of Personal Witness about his own spiritual pilgrimage. But in a few weeks he was back in the old rut, saying that some of us might be gifted with power to win people for Christ, but maybe he was meant for more humdrum activity. There were periods of great depression, self-depreciation. He grew terribly discouraged about his preaching. At times he even wondered whether for him the ministry was not a mistake.

His is a nature of such sensitiveness and fineness of texture that he needs perpetual encouragement from those who are nearest to him. You cannot spoil him; he needs to add the estimate of others to his own under-estimation of himself to be kept anywhere near the truth about himself. For the old pride and snobbery have long since gone by, and given place to the rare grace of genuine humility. It is not easy to preach, whatever it looks like from the pews, and it is still harder to risk the plunge down into the raw of human problems with men one by one. For a long time he remained content with second-best. From that position many men in the ministry never find the challenge, or the way, to extricate themselves.

But later he began to see where the trouble lay. There are three great stages in the spiritual journey of a minister—the initial surrender to God's will, the choice of the ministry, and the forging of a message which will transform lives. He had to be willing to be dissatisfied with merely the kindliness of ordinary pastoral work alone, and with the sort of preaching which leaves people as it finds them, and with living that has no cut to it, no biting edge. He despised the conventional ministry in others; now he must despise it in himself, and be ready to have done with it. It involved a fresh dedication more radical than any that had come before—and his life had been a succession of them.

One afternoon during Holy Week, he talked with two other members of the staff, and got down afresh to bedrock in his life. He bared his small prejudices about them and the rest of us, acknowledging—and so helping to blow away—his small counts against us. There were friendships still hanging over from the old worldly days in college which had never been brought into relation to Christ, so that He might work through them the miracle of regeneration. He told frankly of his fears about himself, his lack of spiritual power, his unwillingness to let God use him to the full. He saw that in reality he was still unsurrendered to the whole of God's possible will for him.

Holy Thursday we had a wonderful service in the evening. It was Gethsemane Night. We thought about our Lord in the agony of the Garden, giving His life anew to God and to the death of the Cross for us. His Spirit was palpably in the place—everyone was conscious of it. We felt we had come somewhere within hearing-distance of His tremendous surrender, " Let this cup pass . . . Nevertheless, not my will, but thine be done."

And that night, right in the middle of the service of the Holy Communion, just at the great moment when he took the cup into his hands to " drink this in remembrance that Christ died for thee," he gave all that was left of his heart to Christ in full and final surrender. It shook him to the very depths of his soul, and it was hard for him to help with the rest of the service. One very near to him saw his face glow like Stephen's.

It took just seven whole years for that man to bring his life completely into line with all he knew of God's will. He faced the issue of surrender first in March, 1920, and he settled it fully in April, 1927. It was a progress studded with periodic reversals to self-erected standards, and requiring repeated rededications to what he knew was right. The decision to enter the ministry did not settle the question for him, ordination did not, the experience of the work of the ministry did not. So long as he consciously withheld from God one portion of his mind and heart, so long was God thwarted in His whole hope for one human life, and for other lives who might have been touched through him. To have stopped anywhere along the line would have been nearly as much an interruption of God's will as to have refused to admit the issue into his mind in the first place. God is always waiting for us to do the very best—and the very best is giving Him everything.

The moment the Great Choice was finally made, all the lesser problems began to clear up. His relation to the rest of the staff became easier, realer, more natural—for the sin of unsurrender walls us off from men as well as from God, and real surrender opens the way to men as it does to God. There came at once into his preaching a new note of the authority of experience; the old tentative, hesitant something was gone.

But chiefly did it change his way with the people about him. He suddenly grew conscious, as though it had not all been " intellectually " known to him all along, of the spiritual potentialities of people he had wholly taken for granted; and blank, dull, static relationships took on creative colour and possibility.

A few days after, he met a young theologue who had not found his feet, who was intellectually at sea, and had no message for needy men. This boy heard him speak at a meeting, and was drawn by the conviction with which the younger man told of his own experience. He came and asked for a talk. Together they strolled away from the meeting for a long walk in the park. At the end of it, the intellectual difficulties had blown away, and this student had given his life to Christ in dead earnest. Word came from him a month after that all worry was gone, and he had begun himself " tackling people."

The curiosity of a young pagan business man was aroused by the assurance with which the young minister spoke of " the only way to live." Human congeniality formed the first basis of acquaintance, but this was only a bridge to get across to more important areas.

Coming back from a short vacation, he had had guidance that he would meet someone on the journey. He met a worldly clergyman, who was drawn to him because he talked a similar language. Clerics often " descend to meet," chatter about viewpoints, or church news, or methods. Not so this time. He waded in from the first, and told him about personal evangelism. All evening they talked together. And when they left, with a wistful, unsatisfied aspiration, the clergyman said, " That is real religion." Laymen do not often realize the needs of a professional minister, or how many ministers lack a definitive experience, or how difficult it is to come to grips with reality about religion in the life of one whose business religion is. To enlist the interest of a man like this, and to hear the expression of his desire for a fuller experience, is a great testimony to power.

One of the men in the choir at Calvary felt a new spirit in this man's preaching and felt attracted to what he had found. They talked casually, and then by appointment. The choir-man went off to relay what he had found. He talked with another member of the choir, a man who had sung in it for eighteen years, during which, he says, " religion ran off me like rain off a duck." He had been married for two years, and he frequently did not go home at night, staying in town to drink and gamble. We had a meeting of choirmen one evening, and there he made a fresh start. He went straight home to make things right with his wife.

The following Sunday he was filled to the brim with enthusiasm, and he must have a talk with this minister. After church he asked whether he could not come and have lunch with him, and the minister told him he would be delighted; for he himself had had guidance not to go out of town for another possible appointment, feeling that someone needed him here. All the afternoon they talked. The choir-man poured out the whole of what had been wrong with him, and listened to the story of the recent transformation of the minister by his own surrender. It may as well be said that the relations between clergy and choir-men are generally formal if not non-existent; and the intimacy of these two men in the things of the Spirit is a fair sight to see. On Thursday the choir-man gave a remarkable testimony in the meeting as to the new lift in his life for six days.

I know of no story in this book which ought to help people more than the story of this man,—aristocratic and somewhat aloof by taste, sensitive, always ready to disbelieve in himself, quickly discouraged, who after long delay and many inconclusive beginnings really found his way. In the early years of his story it almost looked as though God were taking away his liberty and autonomy inch by inch, as though he needed to drive and belabour himself into dedication; but now for the first time, when he has given all without reserve, does he give the impression of entire freedom.   Every phase of his life has been permeated with this new spirit.

It will be a great day for the Christian cause when the world begins to realize that " Thy will be done " does not belong on tombstones, but ought to be graven into the lives of eager men and women who have enlisted in God's warfare beyond return and beyond recall.

XVIII

WANTED—ACTION

L ET us look back a moment—back to the
time when the Master was trying to fashion into a unity that could function spiritually, a little handful of rather nondescript men
whom He had gathered together in His journey
through our world. What did He do with them?
He did not teach them formal theology, nor anything about liturgies and architecture and music
and big books—not but what some of these might
have helped them, but just because other things
came first. He did not make them seem apart
from the common life of the world about them, fit
strange clothes to them, or make them a class by
themselves. He paid attention entirely to the inner side of them. He left out all the modern para-
phernalia, and just kept them close to Himself,
prayed with them, talked with them in the group
and one by one. He trained them in method of
attack, whether upon a village like Capernaum, or
upon an individual like Nathaniel, on whom He
had His eye long before Nathaniel knew it. He
taught them,—not by theory at a distance, but by
doing it,—how to lay siege to a city, or how to get
round a man He wanted to win.

They were a very human and ordinary lot when He took them; and they were a very powerful and extraordinary lot when He was done with them. He taught them two great, simple things: the need of the people, and His own power to satisfy. Nothing else. Nothing professional, nothing of a church system. They learned what was in man, and what He had to correspond to it, as a key fits a lock. Armed with their own discovery of Him, their acquired knowledge of human nature, and a growing conviction that He was the light of all men, they fared forth on their gracious warfare to make the kingdoms His.

Are we making men and women like that? Are the things on which the mind of the Church is characteristically set to-day the same things on which the mind of the apostles was set? Let alone the question of our usefully different means, are we even working really for the same ends? Do you find in the Christians of to-day the same kind of fiery enthusiasm, and burning inward peace, and readiness to say something for the Master, as was in them?

I must confess that I do not. I find the Church busy with the preparation of programmes, elaborately worked out by men sitting behind desks— capable, earnest, executive kind of men, but often men out of touch with the heart-needs of individuals. Sometimes it seems to me a high-minded Confucianist could carry out these plans almost as well as a Christian. The *characteristic* thing about Christianity, the inward, personal transformation of spirit which, at its best, Christianity has always required, is almost entirely wanting. It is assumed, but it is not provided. We ask people to help in carrying out a piece of a plan; but we do not stop to find out whether in their hearts they are committed to the whole plan of Christ for His Kingdom, whether they have taken His way of life for their own. Thousands of church people, taking part in church work, are spiritually unsatisfied, failing in their own homes to get along and to win the members of their family, quarrelling with other church members, spending time over little things which really do not matter to the world, with its bitter heartaches and its desperate need.

Many people like that talk to me, and I know that this is no exaggeration. Some resent and fight against vital personal religion, because it convicts and challenges them to give over their tame little routine for something robust and requiring of energy. But there are many others who are longing for something more absorbing and more satisfying than they are now being given by their churches.

What if we could begin to raise up a new type altogether? Chesterton says of the Franciscan friars that they were " perpetually coming and going in all the highways and byways, seeking to ensure that any man who met one of them by chance should have a spiritual adventure." Suppose we could, with the help of the Spirit, let loose into our country a group of men and women, from every walk of life, caught by the infection of radiant religion, changed and transformed in their own hearts, " seeking to ensure that any man who met one of them by chance should have a spiritual adventure " ? So that when you touched them you got a spark? So that you felt their religion had made them not less human but infinitely more human? So that the world could recover in them something of the astonishing attractiveness which must have been in Christ?

Suppose a few of the ministers and lay-leaders were big enough to admit having been on the wrong track in about nine-tenths of their activity, and having offered people substitutes for the real thing, asking them for the labour of their hands because we had lost the art of asking them for the dedication of their hearts, drawing millions in money from them when we do not know how to draw one confidence, urging them to help us with the spread of a Christianity to the ends of the earth which has not yet reached the recesses of their own hearts— suppose we scrapped some of this terrifying and elaborate machinery, the enormous amount of stuff that is written about financial schemes for churches, and the organization of parishes, and began instead to dig down deep into our own hearts to search ourselves; gave up our ambition and our clerical " side " and our wire-pulling and our party propaganda and our ecclesiastical bickering and our place-seeking and our catering to wealth and big names, and to what the Bishop was going to think if we did something daring, and all the rest of the unholy sham of it, and for once got down to the business of changing lives one by one?

Twelve men rocked the foundations of the world because they gave everything to Christ.

Time does not change the law of that kind of energy.

What could a group on the same basis do to-day? I wonder.

No, I don't wonder—I know perfectly well, and so, gentle reader, do you.

Printed in the United States of America

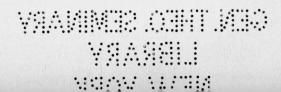